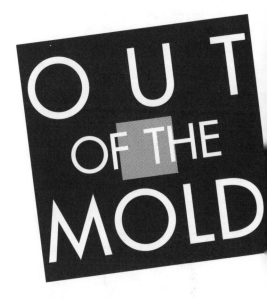

OUT OF THE MOLD

INDEPENDENT VOICES
BREAKING OUT
OF THE MOLD

PUBLISHED IN CELEBRATION OF INDEPENDENT BOOKSELLING
AND
NATIONAL INDEPENDENT BOOKSTORE WEEK

EDITED BY JILL S. PERLSTEIN

AMERICAN BOOKSELLERS ASSOCIATION

CONTENTS

INTRODUCTION

WHEN WE choose to open the pages of a book, we invite a world of experiences into our lives. The written word—in its many forms with its array of individual voices—offers us knowledge and wisdom, brings us hope, makes us laugh and cry, and helps us experience the world more deeply. When we read new authors and explore places and scenes that are so different from our own lives, we broaden our understanding of ourselves and others.

In this collection of writings and illustrations, we celebrate the individual voice and the many ways our lives are enriched and improved through books. Prominent independent booksellers throughout the country have reached out to beloved authors, essayists, poets, journalists, cartoonists, and children's book illustrators with an invitation to join in this collection. Their voices are rich and varied—like the books that fill the shelves of your favorite independent bookstore.

What would it be like if we did not have the freedom to express our independent voices or had more limited access to books? Unimaginable—yet possible, if selection and distribution of information is held in the hands of just a few. A healthy network of locally owned, independent bookstores plays an important role in ensuring a free flow of ideas in our society, which is increasingly dominated by a few large media conglomerates. Diversity, choice, and freedom are what help maintain and nurture the independent creative spirit. *Out of the Mold* reinforces the importance of individual expression, acknowledges that independent minds need independent bookstores, and brings to light the value of sharing our stories.

We hope you will join us in celebrating the efforts of many writers and illustrators who help us expand our worlds—and the independent booksellers who introduce us to the ideas and experiences that keep the creative spirit alive.

—Donna Paz

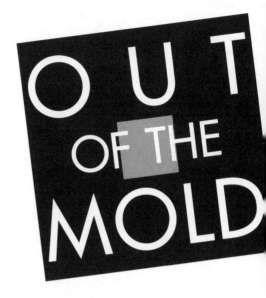

OUT OF THE MOLD

**INDEPENDENT VOICES
BREAKING OUT
OF THE MOLD**

BOOK RACE

BY

PETER SÍS

JANE YOLEN

WHICHEVER

"Whichever Mr. Auden is, I am not."
—*T.S. Eliot*

Whichever Jane Austen is,
I am not;
the minutia of life mystifies me.
Which fork to use,
which spoon,
which side the salad is served,
which the bread
are Elysian mysteries
and Greek to me.
I own no proper gloves.

Whichever Virginia Woolf is,
I am not,
being depressingly and automatically
heterosexual
without calculation.
The place of my own
is my husband's
bourgeois bed.

Whichever Margaret Atwood is,
I am not,
enjoying the company of men,
enjoying the company of women.
Enjoying,
the word as archaic
as most words I prefer:
honesty, compassion, dedication,
a pornography of innocence.

Whichever Sylvia Plath is,
I am not,
life being what I follow,
not death
or the alphabet of guilt
taught in childhood.
I went to Smith
but in a later, sweeter year.

Whichever Jane Yolen is,
that I am,
telling tales that spread out
like hearthsmoke,
sweet and sharp, wood and briar,
stoked by memory
and a strong sense of home.

CONNIE MAY FOWLER

Of Book Tours, Hell, and Possibilities

I HAVE several definitions of hell: anything remotely associated with Jessie Helms, beets, pap smears, Carnival Cruises, being lost at sea or in Newark, parading through a restaurant with toilet paper stuck to my shoe, and—oh yes—author tours. First novelists usually lust after the experience, but that's only because they don't know any better. I asked an author friend if she was going to tour with the paperback publication of her sixth book. She popped a Valium, chased it with a shot of vodka, slammed down the glass, and growled, "Look at me, this is what seven tours have done. I'm staying home."

Typically, by the end of my tours I have gained ten pounds and lost ten years. I weep and mumble—a lot. My second tour was so grueling that by the time I wrote my third novel, *Before Women Had Wings,* I was weeping and mumbling even before the tour began. My agent delicately suggested beta-blockers, my friend the pharmacist, lithium. I have an ingrained fear of pharmaceuticals, so in lieu of taking medication on my tour, I brought my husband. He proved immensely helpful, providing much appreciated company and a calm, steady shoulder for me to lean on. And then the unexpected occurred. As our journey progressed from city to city, bookstore to bookstore, we became aware that we were in the midst of a wondrous phenomenon, one that is as old as storytelling itself, but, unfortunately, is growing ever rarer in this jaundiced age of bottom-line homogenization.

Whether I was reading at Quail Ridge in Raleigh, Northshire Books in Vermont, Charis in Atlanta, Books and Books in Miami, or any of the other nearly thirty stores I visited, the folks who came to hear me read and talk were people whose lives had been profoundly touched, some even changed, by the written word. Their love of books transcended the ordinary for they understood that within those bound pages lies magic: the magic to challenge, to provoke, to build bridges between worlds and races, even to heal the battered spirit. Every time I walked into a bookstore I felt as though I'd entered a temple of ideas, a hallowed space where those ideas could be freely exchanged without fear of retribution or judgment. As the audience and I talked at Mosswood Books in Lakeland, Florida, I thought, this is what church should be like—a celebration of the spirit, independent and diverse and welcoming.

I owe more than I can say to those dear booksellers who have read my work, found it worthy, and then—come hell or high water—put it in the hands of readers. As a writer, I cannot forecast what effect any book I might write will have on an individual. But some people have taken the time to tell me. A woman from St. Augustine wrote to say that someone at her local bookstore, The Booksmith, convinced her to buy *Before Women Had Wings*. Because of the strength of the recommendation, the woman read the book that afternoon. That night she packed her bags, bundled up her baby, and left her abusive husband. "Your book gave me the courage I had been searching for," she wrote. Many women have told me similar stories. I am amazed and privileged that the words I spin sometimes give others such strength. But more than anything, I am grateful that there are booksellers in the world who understand it's not units they are selling, it's possibilities.

I cannot imagine a world without booksellers—and I mean booksellers who take the time to read and appreciate and handsell. They perfectly epitomize the independent spirit, for like latter-day Johnny Appleseeds, they wander through a sometimes indifferent world, spreading the word one book at a time, one reader at a time, never losing faith in that golden myth: a season of grand harvests. By the end of my *Wings* tour, I had gained that dreaded ten pounds, but I had also returned home with a bountiful heart, enriched by the readers and booksellers I had met along the way, knowing that a writer's life is a lonely one but that I've got family out there—one I hope to see on the next tour, a tour that I swear I will not dread.

RICHARD LOUV

Preserving Our Stories

from *The Web of Life: Weaving the Values That Sustain Us*

OUR STORIES, our personal stories, our family stories, are our real gold. If we're lucky, as we age, we put our stories in the bank, where they gather interest in deepening meaning.

"As I grew up, I loved listening to my grandparents' stories," a friend, Liz, told me recently. "I was drawn to their calm and intrigued by the scope of their lives. I remember my grandmother telling stories about my Great-Aunt Ag, who once modeled camisoles and ladies' undergarments."

Today, Liz's family members rarely tell stories.

Somehow we assume that if a story isn't in the video store or on TV, it must not be worth much.

"One evening I was baby-sitting the nine-year-old daughter of a friend. This little girl loves to hear about her mother's life. So she asked me to tell her a story about my childhood, and I was struck with panic. I couldn't think of a thing. I know I have stories. But here was a child asking me for something so simple as a story and I couldn't think of one.

"I learned two things that night. One was that I had lost touch with the stories I grew up with; and two, I'm not making many new stories. Maybe the lives we lead today are mind-numbing, and not the source of many good stories. A lot of the stuff of good stories has to do with family life and we have precious little time for that now."

It's tough to live good stories when you're stuck in traffic.

Author Rexford Brown contends that true literacy is impossible without the ability to value and tell our stories. Brown describes a Navajo school, where one-third of the children come to class illiterate in two languages, English and their native tongue, an indirect, storytelling language that is fading from the culture.

At the reservation he studied, a medicine man stood up at a school board meeting and told a story about twins, one crippled, the other blind: the blind one carries the crippled one, and the crippled one guides them with his eyes; both of them are looking for signs to give their lives meaning and end their wandering. Together, they make their story.

The medicine man went on to attack the schools for neglecting the native language, and for failing to realize that Navajo children have traditionally learned through experience, not books or videos or computers. And he chastised his Navajo people for losing touch with their inheritance of stories and legends.

In a sense, all over America, children are losing their inheritance. They're bused long distances to what amount to educational reservations: schools colonized by bureaucratic story-killing language, schools too often cut off from neighborhood or family. But there are exceptions. "I did find a teacher in Kentucky who created a coal curriculum," Brown says. "He took everything back to square one, and related every part of the class study to coal and to miners: this is what we know. We know coal. Kids need context."

So do the rest of us.

Mental hospitals and our parks are populated with people who have lost their stories or their connection to other people's stories. Nonetheless there seems to be a growing hunger out there. The reaction to the PBS *Civil War* series is an example of how starved people are for powerful, authentic stories about real people, about ourselves and our legacies. And the new popularity of salons— where people get together to do that most radical of acts, talk face-to-face—suggests the hunger.

A college friend, Jewell Scott of Kansas City, told me about a special recent evening, in which her friends' family stories came together. "I was invited to a party to which each person brought their favorite childhood food. The evening began with exclamations over the various dishes—homemade macaroni and real cheese, salmon patties and apple pie and chocolate chip cookies. One dish was cooked right at the party in an authentic, 1960s vintage, Harvest Gold electric skillet."

"What is it?" everyone asked. They peered into the layers of sliced red potatoes with shredded cheese and crumbled bacon, crowned with eggs poaching in the melting cheese.

"It's 'potato stuff,'" the cook responded.

The group reveled in the old-fashioned tastes of real eggs, butter, animal fat, sugar, and cholesterol. After the last apple pie and ice cream had been eaten and they had discussed whether it was better to eat well and live long or eat "good" and die young, the talk returned to their childhoods, their families, and their feelings about them.

Though they had known one another for years, they had never shared these stories, and what they learned was remarkable. "Three of us were descended from circuit-riding ministers who brought the Gospel to the wild Midwest of the mid-to-late 1800s. One grandmother had lived in the northern plains. From Texas to Canada, these great-grandparents we remembered had seen their world change from saddles and shotguns and lonely prairies to electric lights, central air conditioning, and jet travel.

"Our own parents merited our respect for their experiences in the Great Depression and World War II and for rearing their children through a time of incredible rebellion against them and their values. As we sat on the redwood deck, sipping our Chablis and watching a police helicopter cut through the starlit urban sky, we marveled at the legacies they share and how we so rarely talk about them."

The group yearned a bit for the simpler days of "potato stuff" and visits to their grandparents to hear them spin stories of a different time and place. They wondered whether they would live to be eighty or ninety or one hundred, and laughed about how many years the evening's meal had subtracted from their lives.

"And, finally, the evening ended without any conclusion to the most important question: Would we bring to our old age a sense of humor, patience, and kindness that would make us lovable, likable human beings and, someday, thirty or forty or fifty years from now, would there be any reason for another group of party-goers to remember us and our incredible lives?"

When children are asked to define family, they are more forgiving than many adults, and more accurate.

Valeria Lovelace, Sesame Street's *director of research, asked children to define family. Children, in her study, were most likely to identify "Mr. and Mrs. Brown and Billy" as a family. "However, later on in the interviews," says Lovelace, "we said Mr. and Mrs. Brown and Billy live together but they don't love each other. Are they a family?" Half the children who had earlier identified Mr. and Mrs. Brown and Billy as a family now said no, they were not a family. "In the minds of three- to five-year olds, when you say 'family,' they don't just think about a configuration, but an expectation of love and caring as well. When they talk about family, they talk about love. They talk about caring."*

A family can be one mother, or one father, and children; it can be one parent, children, and a network of caring, dependable friends; it can be one child left, the last genetic bearer, grown now, with relatives and ancestors framed and on the wall. Do we wish to tell this man or woman, who has no living relatives left, that he or she has no family? A family exists specifically in the spirit and nowhere else.

JERRY PINKNEY

Illustrations from Minty, A Story of Young Harriet Tubman

AS A conductor on the Underground Railroad, Harriet Tubman led hundreds of slaves, including members of her own family, to freedom in the North. Tubman's daring and heroic efforts against overwhelming odds make her one of the most admired and important women in American history.

In these two portraits from *Minty, A Story of Young Harriet Tubman*, I have tried to give some sense of her strength, independence, and noble spirit, from the age of eight to that of courageous adult.

Illustrations from *Minty, A Story of Young Harriet Tubman*,
written by Alan Schroeder
Dial Books, 1996

JON
SCIESZKA

The Long Lost Fairly
Stupid Tale

THERE ARE some questions in life that it seems we are never meant to know the answer to—How did life begin? Why are we here? What do you call that little groove in the middle of your upper lip?

So it gives me great pleasure and no small excitement to bring you the news that, with the publication of this piece, there will be one less of those ineffable, unanswerable, and annoying questions in this world.

Encouraged by the publishers of this collection to "express oneself freely," I have seized on these pages as a chance to settle the question, once and for all, of what happened to the missing story in *The Stinky Cheese Man and Other Fairly Stupid Tales*.

For those of you not completely tuned in to the world of kids' picture books, *The Stinky Cheese Man* is a book I wrote, Lane Smith illustrated, and Viking published in 1992. *The Stinky Cheese Man* is a book with a lot of unusual features. There is melting type, an endpaper before the end of the book, one completely blank page, and just a lot of generally book-related tomfoolery.

So when I wrote the story of Chicken Licken, I didn't think any of my gentle readers would be too surprised if, when the Table of Contents fell on Chicken

Licken's head, all of the page numbers and one of the stories fell off and did not appear in the book.

How wrong I was.

The first letter appeared within the month of publication.

> Dear Jon Sceizka,
>
> I like your book *The Stinky Cheese Man*. But there is no story in my book called "The Boy Who Cried Cow Patty." Did you forget to put it in?
>
> Your Friend,
> Christine (Age 9)

I wrote Christine a cheerful little note explaining that since the title of the story had fallen off the Contents Page, the story itself had fallen out of the book! Ha ha ha.

The trickle of letters soon turned into a steady stream. And I thought I detected a slight turn in the tone of the letters as well.

> Jon Szkasca,
>
> I am writing to complain about one of your books. The book is called *The Stinky Cheese Man*. The reason I am complaining is cause it is missing a story. "The Boy Who Cried Cow Patty" is not in the book so please send us a new book with the story in it.
>
> Thank-You,
> Alison and Amber

I sent out more of the by now standard replies, ha ha ha, and called my editor to thank her for not letting us print the entire book upside down as we had originally planned.

After I read the next batch of mail, I promised to paint her house and wash her windows every week.

> Mr. Siecskz,
>
> My book is missing "The Boy Who Cried Cow Patty" and I am very mad. Send a good book to me or I will write and tell the publisher of your books.
>
> Really,
> Josh

I wrote little Josh a quick note saying, "When the Table of Contents fell—aw, forget it. Go ahead. Write the publisher. Their address is 375 Hudson Street, NY, NY 10014. And while you're at it, why don't you give Lane Smith a call? Three in the morning would be a good time. Ask him what happened to 'The Boy Who Cried Cow Patty.' Ha ha ha."

My good-humored, "wacky," "zany" facade began to crack. I didn't know if I could take much more. Then came the proverbial letter that broke the hopelessly overextended and pretty well mangled beyond recognition metaphorical camel's back.

> John Szecsiek,
> I do not lik the storey of chiken liken. In the end bcuase it is mising one storey. You are bad. It is wrorng.
> NOT your frind,
> Alex

Sanctuary! Sanctuary! Here is the story of "The Boy Who Cried Cow Patty." Read it. Tell your friends about it. Clip it out and paste it in your *Stinky Cheese* book. But please, please don't write me any more letters about it.

THE BOY WHO CRIED COW PATTY

Once upon a time there was a boy who always cried, "Cow patty!"

He thought this was a great joke.

If someone stepped in mud, the boy would point at their shoe and yell, "Cow patty!" If someone had a stain on their shirt, the boy would yell, "Cow patty!" Whenever anyone smelled a bad smell, the boy would yell, "Cow patty!"

It didn't take long for the whole town to get sick of the boy who was always yelling "Cow patty!"

One day the boy took a shortcut behind Mr. Smith's barn. He didn't know it, but Mr. Smith had just shoveled out his cow barn. So when the boy jumped over the fence without looking, he landed in one gigantic steaming fresh cow patty.

The boy was understandably horrified. He sank up to his neck and kept sinking. He knew that in another minute he would be sunk. So he yelled with all his might, "Fire! Fire! Fire!"

The firemen came rushing to the rescue and found the boy up to his neck in cow patty.

"I don't see any fire," said a fireman. "What are you doing yelling 'Fire'?"

"Well," said the boy. "Nobody would have come if I yelled, 'Cow patty'!"

There. It's done. Printed, published, question answered.

I admit it now, and I think I'm a better writer for it. I was bad. I was wrorng. Now we can all get on with our lives.

But I was just thinking.

Wouldn't it be funny to make a pop-up page that says, "Pull Tab A." Then when you pull Tab A, it just rips out of the book and nothing happens?

Ha ha ha.

DR. JOYCELYN ELDERS & DAVID CHANOFF

Joycelyn Elders, M.D.: From Sharecropper's Daughter to Surgeon General of the United States of America

DURING THE Senate debate over my confirmation as surgeon general in August 1993 some strange things happened. At one point, after Republican senators had been attacking me for awhile, Carol Moseley-Braun, the junior Democrat from Illinois, got the floor. She was mad. She said the debate had turned into lies and character assassination. She said it had become an inquisition and that she didn't know who exactly was vying for the Torquemada Award, but that somebody ought to get it.

When she said that, Don Nickles from Oklahoma stood up and accused her of violating Rule 19, which is the rule against senators slandering other senators. Moseley-Braun hadn't mentioned any names, but Nickles was one of the main ones doing the attacking right then, along with Trent Lott of Mississippi. So Nickles got up and said, "Rule Nineteen." When Ted Kennedy heard that, he called out, "Regular order," meaning that the acting chairman should tell Nickles he was out of order and give the floor back to Moseley-Braun. Then John McCain, the Republican from Arizona, jumped up from where he was sitting on the other side of the aisle, and *he* started yelling, "Regular order!" meaning the chairman should tell Kennedy to sit down and they should get back to Nickles.

I wasn't in the Senate chamber at the time so I didn't see this myself, though it's printed in the *Congressional Record*. According to a friend of mine who was in the gallery, McCain went red in the face and stormed across the way toward Kennedy so angry it looked like he might hit him. When he got there, he said what sounded like "Why don't you shut up, you bully? You're always bossing everybody around," or words to that effect. And Kennedy said, "Why don't *you* shut up?" My friend was wondering what would happen if McCain actually punched Kennedy. Would they somehow be able to turn off the C-Span cameras? Meanwhile the chairman was calling for order and saying, "All senators will suspend!" which meant they had to stop what they were doing and get back to being senators. After that everybody backed off some, but their hackles were still up. Then Phil Gramm from Texas gave a speech that cooled everybody down a little, which gives you an idea how hot they were.

John McCain opposed my confirmation, and Ted Kennedy was fighting hard for me, but they were probably both surprised to find themselves face-to-face like that. McCain is known to get emotional, but he is basically a courteous and friendly man, as I knew from the times I had testified before him earlier. And though conservatives may not like Kennedy's positions, I think everyone sees him as an especially collegial senator. So they might not have recognized themselves in that confrontation.

In a lot of the controversy over my nomination I could scarcely recognize myself. What people might have thought who didn't know me but only read the newspapers I can't even begin to imagine.

At one point in the debate Ted Kennedy had said they were going to be voting on the real Joycelyn Elders, not some unrecognizable straw woman. But when it was over, I wasn't positive people knew who I was much better than they had when it started. After only fifteen months as surgeon general, I'm not sure they ever really did get to find out.

The town of Schaal, Arkansas, where I was born on August 13, 1933, has a population of ninety-eight, ninety-nine when I'm home. Schaal is too small for most maps, especially since the Williams brothers' general store burned down and the post office moved to Mineral Springs. The only other enterprises in town were the cotton gin and a little ground hog sawmill, and they too are long gone.

To get to Schaal, you take the interstate west out of Little Rock. The moment you branch off onto Route 24, you're deep in the country. The white oak and pine woods look just like they did in my childhood. So do the fenced pastures with their little knots of cattle. When the more prosperous farms near the interstate give out, you begin to see wooden shacks and churches—tiny white buildings scattered along the highway at quicker intervals than you might expect. The churches aren't much bigger than the houses. The only real difference is there's a steeple on top and a name over the door: Sweet Home Baptist, Calvary Methodist, AME Zion, Church of Christ, Assembly of God, Church of God in Christ.

Heading toward Nashville and Mineral Springs, you feel like you're going back to an earlier time. On Sundays the churches are full. If you turn off the air conditioning in your car and open the windows, you can hear snatches of singing as you drive by. All along Route 24 the air is humming with old hymns.

Nashville, not the big one in Tennessee, but the little one near Schaal, is where the black kids from the farms used to go on special occasions when I was young. You saved your pennies and Edmund Turner came around in his battered bus and picked you up, the same bus he used to take children to school and workers out to migrant labor jobs picking cotton in Arizona or tomatoes in Ohio. In Nashville we'd walk around staring in the store windows and maybe see a movie at the Rialto—from up in the balcony in those days of segregation. That was a once- or twice-a-year thing. That was our idea of a good time, strolling the sidewalks, getting a Popsicle or a soda, checking out everybody else, even if half of them were your cousins to one degree or another. You saved up hard for that.

Drive down the winding dirt road toward Schaal, and you are about as far from Washington, D.C., as you can get. If you're from here and old enough like I am to remember before tractors and electrification, the surprise is how little it's changed. It takes no trouble at all to picture in your imagination large families working in the fields, children and adults together, everyone trooping back home at sundown to bathe in the round tin tubs that were set out on the back porch all day so the water could catch the heat of the sun. That's what I did from the time I could walk in the furrows until the day I left home for college when I was sixteen. I'd throw my sweated-through, dirt-caked field dress in the washpot for boiling and blueing; then I climbed into a tub and scrubbed hard. The idea wasn't just to get clean; it was to kill off the ticks and chiggers that might have gotten through your clothes and started looking for some nice warm spot to burrow in. If you didn't get them in time, next day you'd be nothing but a giant welt.

To see the actual places where I grew up, a car won't do. You need to go by pickup truck. Both the houses of my childhood are gone now, the Ollie Reed place and the Old Wes Jones place. All that's left of them are little flattened rises in the middle of overgrown meadows that used to be full of cotton and corn. But the landmarks are still there, like the big sweet gum tree. We used to take lunch in its shade, Mama and Daddy coming up from the fields they were working, me and the other children coming in from ours. The tree gave off a sap you could chew like gum.

Go down beyond the gum tree toward the bottom, and you're walking through what used to be our big stand of sugarcane. You can't see any traces of that anymore. But the pear tree is still heavy with fruit, even though it's hedged in by other trees that sprouted up after we left. Not far from there our old overflowing well is bubbling out a steady stream of water, the same as always. That was our main source at the Ollie Reed place. It was wonderful, clear water, which we appreciated a lot more after we moved to Wes Jones. But it was a good quarter mile from the house, which made hauling the buckets a hard task.

Off behind the well in a thicket is the old family cemetery where many of Mama's people are buried. It's uncared for now and overgrown. It's in the process of returning to nature. Right next to it is the remains of an even older cemetery, long abandoned even when I was a child. We think it was a burial ground of the Joneses. They were one of the early white families in Schaal and still big landowners by local standards when we farmed the land. We knew them all well, especially Miss May Dorsey, a Jones daughter who lived up the lane from us. Her boy Glenn Dean played with my brothers, and she and Mama helped each other out when babies were sick or other emergencies came up, which they did regularly.

By contrast with the overflowing well, our dug well near the house was shallow and brackish. At times the surface got a kind of green scum on it, and it wasn't all that unusual for the whole family to come down with stomach distress and diarrhea. The same was true for the Old Wes Jones place, where we moved when I was twelve. Wes Jones didn't even have a privy, though I suppressed that memory for years. But I do have a sharp recollection of the privy behind the Ollie Reed house. That place frightened me every time I had to use it. Especially the screwworms that crawled around in there, big and fat as a small snake.

Whenever my mother's reading lessons got too confusing for me, I used to run and hide behind that privy. "Now you tell me," Mama would say, "what happens when you put that *e* after the word? What's that make it?" This is one of my first clear memories. I could read the word fine. I just had. It was "c-a-p, cap." But my four-year-old brain was having a hard time getting itself around the final *e* idea. Out of the corner of my eye I could see the switch in Mama's hand beginning to bounce a little. She'd tan the back of my legs with that if my progress slacked off too much. Mama's switching wasn't meant to hurt, but it stung enough so I wanted to avoid it. "I got to go, Mama. I got to go bad. I'll be right back." And I'd race out to the privy and stand behind it, not wanting to duck inside, because of the worms, but not wanting to go back to the house either. I'd wait it out as long as I could, hoping that she'd start doing something else and forget about the lesson. But she never would. "You got to learn your letters, honey, and your numbers. You've got to get a good start."

"You've got to get a good start!" I think she said that as often as she said prayers. Mama was a small, wiry woman, always smiling, always with a good word for everyone and a heartful of love. A wonderful, giving-of-herself kind of person. She never looked at the negative side of things, either then or until she passed last year at age eighty-three. She was always a sunny optimist, even when there was precious little to be optimistic about. Even when things were horrible, she always thought that she was just the luckiest woman in the world. "I'm so grateful all my children are healthy and nothing's wrong with them," she'd say. "I just feel rich."

Mama's name was Haller. She was born Reed, which became Jones when she and Daddy, Curtis Jones, got married secretly. She was eighteen, and he was nineteen, so they weren't children. But the families hadn't been told, much less asked. So it wasn't smooth. Mama was on the girls' basketball team at school, and the story goes that she came home on the bus in her basketball uniform. But instead of going inside to do her after-school chores she ran off in her shorts to meet Daddy and get to the preacher. Those who remember say that Haller's daddy, my grandpa Charlie Reed, was so mad he went looking for his new son-in-law with a shotgun. He calmed down later, though I always had a sense that Daddy's family might have been happier with the match than Mama's was.

In those days school went only part-time since all the students worked regularly on the farm. As a result, extremely few of them graduated, and all of them were older for their grade level than is common nowadays. Mama finished the eighth grade herself, which was pretty good for a black woman growing up in the southwestern corner of Arkansas in the first part of the century. And she had a tremendous determination that all her children were going to be educated. She didn't ease off any on the seven that came after me. But as her first I experienced that determination at its fiercest.

It wasn't that Mama had any particular aspirations for us, like becoming a doctor or lawyer or professor. Professions like that were outside our world. Going to college wasn't something that ever occurred to any of us. The only thing we ever saw people doing was work; I'm talking hard physical labor. The only time we ever saw anybody in a suit was in church. Everybody we knew was in overalls driving mules. But somehow Mama held tight to the conviction that if we ever wanted to "be something," we had better get educated.

"Being something" might have been on Mama's tongue a lot, but it wasn't something I ever particularly thought about. I did sometimes fantasize about becoming a store clerk. To be a clerk in a ten-cent store or a grocery store would have been a real improvement, particularly when the temperature in the fields got up around a hundred and the mosquitoes were swarming and the humidity made the air so thick you could all but see it. Days like that, being a clerk in some kind of cool, dim store seemed like it might be a good way to spend your life. Clerks didn't plow fields or weed furrows. They didn't chop cotton or strip cane or bale hay from sunup to sundown. The only problem was that no store clerk I had ever seen was black. Around Schaal, indoor work was white. Except for maids. Maids worked inside, but maid work didn't exactly seem like "being something."

By the time I was five I was well prepared for school. By then I was already a good reader, which allowed Mama to go to work on my sister Katie, who was two years younger than I. I had long outgrown the primer Mama used for lessons and had taken to reading the Bible, which was the other book in the house. My brother Chester, who's a Methodist minister now, tells everyone that the reason he went into the church is that the Bible was the only book we had around for him to read. It was my only book too, and though I didn't become a minister, more than once I've had people accuse me of preaching. I also pored over the weekly *Grit*, a farmers' newspaper out of Kansas that Daddy subscribed to. When I finally started first grade at Bright Star school, I was astonished to find I could always get some kind of book there, like *Grimm's Fairy Tales*. Not only that, but I could take it home and read at night after everything that had to get done had gotten done. I'd prop a blanket on the floor like a tent, put a coal-oil lamp under it, and curl up with Hansel and Gretel.

Katie and I slept in one bed in the second of our three rooms, where we were soon joined by our brothers Charles and Bernard. After that my parents took a little rest before they started having Chester, Beryl, Pat, and Phillip. Being the oldest automatically made me the work leader and the baby nurse. But I don't really remember ever taking care of Katie. I always felt like she was helping me, whereas Charles and Bernard and the others I was constantly looking after. Mama would have the new baby, and I'd have the rest.

Katie was my friend and companion in helping keep the house and farm going. I did whatever I could for my age, and Katie followed right behind me, doing everything she could: drag a bucket, scrub clothes, haul a little water from the well. In the morning we got up as soon as we heard Mama and Daddy stirring. Then we started in on the chores that had to get done before school time, first of all building the fire, then slopping the hogs.

Because water had to be brought up from a distance, we used it sparsely. Even the used dishwater got saved in a big five-gallon can by the back door, which was also where we threw all the leftover kitchen scraps. Whatever was in that can went for the hogs. Daddy also bought something called shorts, a kind of coarse reddish gray meal that we kept out in the smokehouse. Every morning first thing Katie and I would bring in a bagful of shorts and mix it up with the slops. Then she'd get on one side of the can and I'd get on the other. We'd both grab the handle, trying to get a little of the wooden middle of it so we wouldn't hurt our hands as much, and we'd carry and drag it out to the pen and pour it in the trough.

We might have had six or seven hogs in the pen, and while we were pouring, they would crowd in and start eating. They would be all around us, snuffling and grunting. Some of them must have weighed four hundred pounds, but big as they were, we didn't have any fear of them. You could push on them and they'd move. Hit them on the head and they'd back up.

The slop would never be enough, so we'd have to get a batch of dried corn from the barn and throw some of that to them too. I don't remember ever having too much of a personal relationship with pigs. We had some cows we had more of a friendship with, but not pigs.

Once the hogs were done, the cows had to be milked. Oftentimes we'd have to go get them from the pasture and bring them down into the barn. Though I don't remember exactly, I think my aunts and uncles on my mother's side must have taught me how to milk. Grandpa Charlie Reed owned lots of cows, and he and his children milked them. They sold milk and cream. My uncles Slim and Bone and Dr. Tom and Aunt Suzy and Uncle Buh—Buddy—would milk twenty or thirty cows twice a day.

At our house we had only four or five cows. Katie and I would go get them with a little stick and herd them in. Small as we were, there was no problem. Cows herd pretty easily. We'd get them into the barn, then let their calves in to them so they could suck a little. The calves' sucking made the milk let down into the teats. When the calves had sucked some, we'd put a rope around them and pull them over to the fence, where we tied them up so they couldn't get back at the cows. Then we could start milking. Without the calves stimulating the letdown, milking would have been too hard for us. But once the milk came down, it was easy as pie. All it needed was gentle pulling. Besides, if you did it too hard, the cow would kick you. We were always careful not to take all the milk, though. You had to leave some for the calves after.

We milked those cows every day, but I never did become a champion milker. I always held my bucket with one hand while I milked with the other. I was afraid to put the bucket on the ground because I thought the cow might kick it over. So I was never brave enough to use both hands and go full speed, the way Aunt Suzy and Uncle Buh taught me to do.

When we were finished milking, we hauled the big milk canister back in the house and strained it. We used a clean sheet for that, to make sure that any extraneous material wasn't in there. After we strained it, we covered it up in what we called the milk bucket and set it out on the back porch to clabber—that is, to ferment. We'd let it clabber; then we'd churn butter and buttermilk later on. Regular milk would go bad in a day, but buttermilk kept.

By the time we were finished chores the sky would be lightening and Mama would have breakfast ready. Usually she'd make rice and biscuits, ham or salt meat, and always something sweet, like molasses bread and jam. She'd cook enough for breakfast and lunch both. Then we'd all sit down at the big table and say grace. "Good Lord, we thank Thee for the blessings we are about to receive for the nourishment and strength of our bodies, for Christ's sake. Amen."

Just in front of our house was a little creek branch. When I started school at Bright Star, I'd wait for the kids from the four or five houses below us to come by, maybe six of us all together. The branch crossed the road, and Daddy used to lay down planks over it. But every time it rained the branches would pool and the planks would wash away. So we'd wade it or jump. Either way everybody's shoes would get sopped, and we'd walk to school with wet feet.

I always walked with Clara Dean Davis, who was my best friend and in the same grade as I was. We'd take the muddy trail a couple of miles through the woods until we reached the main road, talking all the way. Usually it was about dolls or what we were doing in school or the houses we'd have when we grew up. Nice, big houses. By that we meant bigger than the unpainted three-room shacks we both lived in. By nice we thought about windows that weren't broken and covered with cardboard or a roof that didn't leak in a dozen places. We didn't dream of electricity. We didn't know about it, so we didn't miss it. Nobody had electricity, or indoor plumbing either. Neither of us had seen a real bathtub.

Bright Star was really just a wide place in the road. There was a store and a pasture across the road that the men kept cleared so they could play baseball on Saturday afternoons. Then there was Bright Star elementary, where we went. Bright Star elementary was painted white. It had two rooms and a kind of recessed alcove where the front door was that we could stand under if it rained during lunch or recess. In the middle of the room was a potbellied stove. All the kids sat on long wooden benches. There were no desks, just benches. I'm pretty certain the white schools had desks at that time, given the way things were. But we worked on our laps on big sheets of paper we'd tear off a tablet.

Our teacher, Miss Ulistine Brown, taught a roomful of kids who might have ranged in age from five to thirteen. Since we didn't have workbooks, she'd write out our lessons on the board and we'd copy them on to our paper. She would have one group doing numbers, another writing, and a third doing something else—all at the same time. Thinking back on it, I know that classroom must have been a noisy place, but I don't remember any of us noticing. When you lived in a house where there might be four or eight or ten children, there wasn't all that much difference.

Shortly after I got home from school each day, we'd eat supper. Daddy would come in from working, and we'd all sit down around the long kitchen table. Everybody always ate together, no matter what. Later on, when I had my own family, that was still important to me. But back then it was survival. If you had eight kids and you were fixing three meals a day, no one had any choice. If you fixed it and someone wasn't there to eat, that person didn't get any. So you never had a problem getting people to the table. It was all served family style in big bowls: the peas and butter beans and fried corn and squash and ham and whatever else was ready in the garden or Daddy had hunted, all depending on the season.

I'd talk while we ate, about what had happened in school, what I had learned, or who might have done what to whom. Katie and Charles and the others would be babbling too. But it was mainly Mama who carried the conversation with us. Daddy mostly talked when someone got out of hand. Even then he'd limit himself to something like "Didn't y'all hear your mother?" I never had the feeling that he wasn't interested in us; he just wasn't given to words. The only real talking he was going to do was when you came in from working a section of field. Then he'd ask how it went, or how much you had got chopped, or if you had any trouble with the mule. It was not what you would call an actual conversation per se.

The fact was that Daddy was consumed by work. Mama labored side by side with him in the fields, but she also took care of the garden and the cooking and the house and of course the baby. The eight of us were spread out over eighteen years, which meant she was either pregnant or nursing for most of that time. But Daddy's life was on the land. From spring through fall he was always plowing, planting, chopping, picking, cutting, or baling. In the winter he hunted and trapped, raccoon mainly, but also possum and squirrel and wild mink.

Sometimes he and a few of his friends would get their dogs together and go after a fox. But his serious hunting he did by himself, and that was most of the time. Hunting for Daddy was work. Selling hides to Sears and Montgomery Ward was one of the few cash-money sources he had. He'd hunt coons with the dogs he bought from a breeder in Paducah, Kentucky, all of them with papers. He prided himself on those dogs. Most people we knew had dogs that were maybe half hunting dog, half stray mongrel. But for Daddy a good coon dog was an investment. His sweat was going mainly into sharecropping other people's land, which was what we were doing on the Old Wes Jones place. But he used the raccoon money to start buying up land for himself, a little section at a time. It took years, but eventually he had eighty acres of his own, most all of it bought with coonskins.

One winter my little brother Bernard got sick. First he started complaining that his stomach hurt him, which nobody paid that much attention to. Stomach ailments weren't exactly uncommon in our house. It could have been something in the water, or maybe he had eaten some green apples, which was a favorite explanation for stomachaches. I didn't doubt that he really might have eaten some green apples. Bern was about the most rambunctious four-year-old you could ever imagine, always getting into a mess or fighting with Charles or climbing on things. You could tell him not to eat green apples a hundred times and he'd go and eat the first one he could locate. But then he started running a fever, and nothing Mama gave him would stay down. After he started throwing up, he wouldn't take anything at all. He just lay there with his eyes wide open, saying, "My stomach hurts."

That night I listened to Bernard whining softly and grunting like a little pig in the bed he shared with Charles across the room from Katie and me. "Unh, unh, unh," all night long. Next day his stomach started to swell up. Mama had put a kind of loose gown on him, probably somebody's shirt, and I sat next to him on the bed, sponging him off, trying to get the fever to go down. I mopped his forehead and his chest and his skinny little legs. But it wasn't helping. It looked to me like his stomach was bulging out. When I touched it, it was hard as a rock. Mama kept coming in from the kitchen to look. "Oh, my," she said. "We can't just let him lay there like this. Oh, my, we just got to get my baby to the doctor."

I was nine then, and that was the first I had ever heard Mama say anything about going to a doctor. In Schaal, if somebody got sick or hurt, people didn't necessarily associate that with going to doctors. Doctors cost money, and for the most part Schaal didn't run on a money economy. Besides, the nearest one was a white doctor twelve miles away. That meant a day there and back if you didn't have a car, which almost no one did. So that twelve miles might as well have been a thousand.

I had watched my aunt Mary die of meningitis, her neck stretched out and her back arched up. My grandpa Charlie Reed had also died not too long before, of appendicitis. Neither of them had seen a doctor. No more than Mama had when she had her babies or my schoolmate little Val Belcher had when he was kicked in the head by a mule at the age of four and left palsied and crippled. The beginning and end of my understanding on the subject were that if you got sick or something happened to you, either you pulled through or you died. There wasn't much else.

So when Daddy came in from hunting that night, I was surprised to hear Mama tell him he had to take Bernard to the doctor. "Well," said Daddy. I could tell he wasn't prepared for what Mama had said and he needed to think about it. Daddy might have respected Mama most often, but he didn't always worry too much about doing what she said to do. But Mama was determined to save Bernard if she could. "Curtis," she said, "if this child makes it through till morning, you have got to take him."

I don't know what Mama and Daddy thought, but I guessed that Bernard was probably going to die that night. He was usually such a chatterbox, but now he wasn't saying a word. All night long I listened in the dark. I could make out Charles's regular breathing, but there was no sound from Bernard, except for a little grunt every now and then.

The next morning when I woke up and went over to look, Bernard wasn't moving. But I could feel his chest rising and falling, and he grunted a couple of times, though much softer now than last night. Daddy was already out in the lot getting the mule ready, and Mama was at the stove cooking something up for him. It was obvious she wasn't thinking about a thing except getting him and Bernard off. After Daddy ate, he put on his hunting coat, the heavy brown one with the corduroy collar and all the little pockets for his shotgun shells. Then he held a blanket while Mama picked Bernard up and wrapped him into it. When Daddy took him, Bernard's head fell back, and he winced from the pull on his swollen stomach. "You got to hold his head up, Curtis," said Mama. "Hold his head up so he don't hurt so bad."

I watched Daddy go out and get on the mule. It looked like he had rigged up something in front of the saddle to rest Bernard on while they were riding. Then Mama and I stood and watched as he turned the mule around and went across the branch. We watched them pass the house up the road where Miss Grace and Mr. Sleety lived and go on around the bend. Then they disappeared behind the cottonwoods.

It wasn't till late at night that we heard the mule come back. When we went out to see, there was Daddy sitting on Old Jim holding Bernard in his arms, still bundled up in the blanket. Bernard looked the same as when he had left, huge-eyed and silent as death. But when we took the blanket off, I saw a big red tube sticking out of his stomach. The doctor had told Daddy Bernard's appendix had burst. He put the big red tube in there to drain the poison out of him. Then he sent them home. There were no hospitals around there for any black children.

I see so much of the traditional portrait of America in the things that I have known in my life. The farm and the little country church, a loving mother and father who spent every ounce of their strength to feed their family and who watched their children rise from poverty to college and good jobs. All that could have come straight out of Norman Rockwell. Except that my American dream was in color.

I was among the first generation of African Americans who could even think about saying "my American dream." And even for me that was more a matter of luck than anything else. Once I got to medical school, I made it the way young white men traditionally did, by having a mentor who took a real interest in me and did what needed to be done to promote my career. But it was just my good fortune that I came along at the particular moment I did.

If I had come up ten years earlier, I never would have been picked to be chief pediatric resident at the University of Arkansas, or any resident. Chances are I never would have gotten into medical school at all. Ten years earlier black students in the South could go only to black medical schools. With just two, Meharry and Howard, it was almost impossible to get admitted. And if you did get in, there was almost no way to go from there into academic medicine. Those schools provided excellent clinical training, but they didn't have the resources to do much high-level medical research. The world of medical science would have been closed to me. I might have set up a practice in a black community or inner city and been a good doctor. But I never would have had the opportunities I did, never would have done the science and medicine I did, never would have had the life I've led.

But I came along at a time when some universities were beginning to take black students, even trying to recruit. With almost no black faculty members, medical schools were just starting to look for young African Americans to go into academic medicine. And I had the right bag of tricks for that moment: a feel for science, an ability to get along with people, and a determination not to fail. There was no affirmative action then, but a broad cultural change was under way. Fortunately for me I was there at the right time.

Some years later that social momentum got translated into the policy of affirmative action. Now twenty-five years have gone by, and there's a backlash. People want to get rid of affirmative action, nobody more than the social conservatives.

Their main argument is that affirmative action should be scrapped because it supposedly favors unqualified blacks over qualified whites. We have a level playing field now, they argue, so why prolong such a racially divisive policy?

Well, I can tell you that most African Americans do not see affirmative action that way. We look at a history in this country of education and jobs going to white people simply because they were white, while untold numbers of talented black people were disregarded and swept aside. We see a playing field that for almost all this country's existence was not just slanted against blacks; they weren't even allowed on it so they could get into the game.

That's first. Secondly, the group affirmative action has helped most is not blacks but white women. I'm not saying that's bad. Far from it. Women have suffered their own long experience of exclusion from America's promises. When I served on the admissions committee at the medical school, I had to spend more time shouting to get women admitted than I did to get blacks in. But though women have been the chief beneficiaries of affirmative action, we never hear talk about how destructive the policy is to relations between the sexes, only to those between the races.

Most important, although nobody ever talks about it, the real significance of affirmative action is not that it advantages one group or another, but that it is medicine designed to cure America's ailing institutions. Historically the country's colleges, professional schools, businesses, and unions have been sick. They discriminated against minorities and women in favor of white men. In their prejudice they deprived themselves of the full available pool of talent, which hurt them, those they excluded, and the country they were meant to be serving.

Because their discrimination was embedded for so long, these institutions have needed help in healing themselves. The civil rights movement created a climate that allowed some of society's second-class citizens to go where they had previously been kept out. A few in my generation were able to swim the river. But the institutions themselves remained flawed at the center, despite their attempts to do better. Given that they were founded by white males to benefit white males and that their culture has always been a white male culture, how could it be different?

Changing institutions is a long-term business. Four hundred years of affirmative action in favor of white males have not been successfully countered by a twenty-five-year attempt to make sure minorities and women are included. That's why affirmative action is still needed. Habits die hard, even where the spirit is willing to change. Equality and fairness don't happen in the blinking of an eye. They take root slowly.

Maybe some people think we're there already. I don't. Look at the upper levels of management today, and you'll see that blacks and women barely exist. The same with upper-level faculty at today's law, business, and medical schools. Someone the other day showed me a photograph from the Boston *Globe*, the most liberal state's most liberal newspaper, a picture of ten women CEOs. If fairness had already dug itself deep into our institutions, we would never see such a picture. If equality were the norm, we'd never hear about this black professor or that black banker. They'd be too common to notice.

When affirmative action has done its job, it will wither away. No one will have to kill it because it will die its own natural death. Voting rights laws are not needed where everyone has the right to vote. Affirmative action makes no sense where institutional prejudice does not exist. But if you think we are already there, just look around.

All this having been said, the truth is that affirmative action is a philosophy that goes deeper than race, deeper than gender, and beyond institutions. It goes right to the heart of our democratic life.

No matter how wide the doors have swung, if you can't read, you're not going through. Thirty years ago we saw that the doors were closed and had to be opened. Now we know that so many of our youngsters will never be prepared to step through. White and black, boys and girls, it makes no difference. Sixty-five percent of our poor and ignorant and underserved are white. White and black, they grow up in places where so often there's nobody to read them a book, nobody to see they do their homework, nobody to make sure they're fed properly or clothed decently. We can't wait for these children to get old enough to look for a job or think about college before we apply affirmative action. By then it's too late, for them and for us.

That's why I argue everywhere I go that resources have to be focused on our children—on Head Start and early enrichment and after-school programs. I want to be saying to this country something more than just "Yes, I made it, so you can too." Because the fact is that I had plenty of help: a stable family, a working community, teachers who cared, and a church that mattered. But this kind of help is not out there for so many of today's young people growing up in broken homes and broken communities. In a country as rich as ours we all have an obligation to do everything we can to try to balance this out, so these children too can have a chance to cross the river and see what it's like on the other side.

That's how I see a lot of what I've tried to do. In my own way I've done what I could to keep them healthy, to get them through school, and to give them hope. That's what I wanted for all those children I saw in the delta and up in Arkansas's mountains, the ones who were in my care when I was health director and the ones who came into my care when I was surgeon general. If I could keep them well, keep them from having children while they were still children themselves, and give them some hope they could go to college, that's what I wanted. That was my idea of affirmative action. After they got past that, they could take care of themselves.

When it comes right down to it, I don't really think of myself as a model for young black women. If anything, I hope to be some kind of example for disadvantaged young people of all kinds, for the kids who don't have the usual models they should be growing up with. I want us—you and I—to think of all those kids as our children. That's what I really want. When you pare away all the excess and get down to the core, that's what I am about.

This is an excerpt from Joycelyn Elders, M.D.: From Sharecropper's Daughter to Surgeon General of the United States of America.

ANNE LAMOTT

Finding Your Voice

from Bird by Bird: Some Instructions on Writing and Life

I HEARD a tape once in which an actor talked about trying to find God in the modern world and how, left to our own devices, we seek instead all the worldly things—possessions, money, looks, and power—because we think they will bring us fulfillment. But this turns out to be a joke, because they are just props, and when we check out of this life, we have to give them all back to the great propmaster in the sky. "They're just on loan," he said. "They're not ours." This tape changed how I felt about my students emulating their favorite writers. It helped me see that it is natural to take on someone else's style, that it's a prop that you use for a while until you have to give it back. And it just might take you to the thing that is not on loan, the thing that is real and true: your own voice.

I often ask my students to scribble down in class the reason they want to write, why they are in my class, what is propelling them to do this sometimes-excruciating, sometimes-boring work. And over and over, they say in effect, "I will not be silenced again." They were good children, who often felt invisible and who saw some awful stuff. But at some point they stopped telling what they saw because when they did, they were punished. Now they want to look at their lives—at life—and they don't want to be sent to their rooms for doing so. But it is very hard to find their own voice and it is tempting to assume someone else's.

Every time Isabel Allende has a new book out, I'm happy because I will get to read it, and I'm unhappy because half of my students are going to start writing like her. Now, I love Ms. Allende's work, as I love a number of South and Central American writers. When I read their books, I feel like I'm sitting around a campfire at night where they are spinning their wild stories—these crazy Rube Goldberg clocks, with lots of birds and maidens and gongs and bells and whistles. I understand why this style is so attractive to my students: it's like primitive art. It's simple and decorative, with rich colors, satisfying old forms, and a lot of sophistication underneath that you feel but don't really see. I always feel like I'm watching a wild theater piece with lots of special effects—so many lives falling apart! But, more important, this style offers the nourishment of imagination and wonder. I love to enter into these fantastical worlds where we feel like we're looking through the wrong end of the binoculars, where everything is tiny and pretty and rich, because real life is so often big and messy and hurtful and drab. But when someone like Allende polishes and turns and twists her people and their lives and their families and their ghosts into universal curves and shapes, then the writing resonates in such a way that you think, Yes, yes, that's exactly what life is like.

I love for my students to want to have this effect. But their renditions never ring true, any more than they ring true a few months later when Ann Beattie's latest book arrives and my students start submitting stories about shiny bowls and windowpanes. We do live our lives on surfaces, and Beattie does surfaces beautifully, burnishing them, bringing out the details. But when my students do Beattie, their stories tend to be lukewarm, and I say to them, Life is lukewarm enough! Give us a little heat! If I'm going to read about a bunch of people who drive Volkswagens and seem to have mostly Volkswagen-sized problems, and the writer shows them driving around on top of the ice, I want a sense that there's a lot of very, very cold water down below. I eventually want for someone to crash through. I want people who write to crash or dive below the surface, where life is so cold and confusing and hard to see. I want writers to plunge through the holes—the holes we try to fill up with all the props. In those holes and in the spaces around them exist all sorts of possibility, including the chance to see who we are and to glimpse the mystery.

The great writers keep writing about the cold dark place within, the water under a frozen lake or the secluded, camouflaged hole. The light they shine on this hole, this pit, helps us cut away or step around the brush and brambles; then we can dance around the rim of the abyss, holler into it, measure it, throw rocks in it, and still not fall in. It can no longer swallow us up. And we can get on with things.

Ha Ha the Cat

1968 WAS a time of great change for me. I was at a turning point in my life. In the last year I had dropped out of my junior year of college in San Francisco, been beaten up by strangers and left for dead, and had broken up with Linda, the first girl I really loved.

I moved to Santa Barbara a few hours away from Linda, in Santa Monica. I wanted to be close enough to win her back, but not too close, in case I couldn't. I had no friends or contacts in Santa Barbara, but it felt like a good place to heal.

A psychiatrist and his wife hired me as a live-in gardener at their home in the hills overlooking the town. All I knew about gardening was how to grow tomatoes and mow lawns, but I was willing to learn what I needed to know. There were no lawns to mow at the doctor's house, but there were roses, hundreds of roses. That's what sold me on the job—my lack of money and the smell of roses.

The apartment they gave me was perfect. It was separate from the main house but attached to the office where the doctor saw his patients. It was a plain, small place, filled with light and surrounded by roses. Inside there was a single bed, a lamp, a desk where I wrote love letters to Linda, an odd painting of Switzerland, and a small kitchen. I didn't need anything more. Since I had been hitchhiking around for a few months, I had very few things of my own. Just some clothes, an old guitar my Dad had given me which neither of us had learned to play, a copy of *Siddhartha*, and John Lomax's book, *Cowboy Songs*.

It was the first time in my twenty-two years that I had ever lived alone and I had a lot to sort out. I hadn't even spoken to my parents in the year since I had been out of college. My girl was gone, and I had no idea about what to do with my life.

Tending the roses became my solace. The doctor's wife taught me how to be a nursemaid, care giver, and wrangler to several hundred roses. The roses taught me how to be quiet, alone, and attentive. They were my herd. A big healthy herd, with names like Mister Lincoln, Golden Glow, Whiskey Mac, King's Ransom, Blue Girl, and Helen Hayes. There were also old-time roses and some five-petaled ones with names like Fantin-Latour, Nasturana, and Swamp Rose.

Roses need constant attention and a lot of work. In California they need to be watered every other day, at sunup, so the sun won't scorch the leaves. The goal is to not get water on the plants at all, because the water droplets act like tiny magnifying glasses, burning the petals and leaves. We had to fertilize each plant, aerate the soil, give each plant a gallon of fish emulsion, test the soil and spread lime, spray to control black spot, mildew, and rust, and constantly prune and, of course, get rid of the ever-present Japanese Beetle.

The doctor's wife preferred to have me pick the bugs off by hand. I guess I've handled more Japanese Beetles than anyone on the face of the earth. This was a never-ending job, but good work for a man with no social life.

Early evening is when you get quality time with roses. They seem to settle into a quiet sensuousness. Their subtle shades of pink, red, lavender, yellow, and creamy white lit by the incredible California sunsets seemed to be nature's way of saying, All is well. The roses open up, become vulnerable, and send out their luscious, sweet smells.

Afterwards I would go back to my little room and cook supper. I was a vegetarian at the time and ate a steady diet of brown rice, vegetables, tofu, and miso soup.

The only thing dividing my kitchen from the psychiatrist's office was a plywood door. Patients would come to his office while I was cooking supper, and I could hear almost every word. At first I was surprised and slightly embarrassed, but since I had no TV, record player, or even a radio, this became my evenings' entertainment.

A patient and his wife would come in. He: "She never gives me enough sex." She: "Are you kidding? You are driving me crazy with all the sex." Doctor: "How often do you have it?" He: "Twice a week." She: "I read the Kinsey report, and every man in there said he wasn't getting enough sex. This is not just my problem." He: "I'm thinking about leaving." She: "I don't know if I want to stay." They go around and around. Finally the hour is up and the doctor gives them some advice, closing with: "There are two ways to get to the top of an oak tree. You can climb the branches, or sit on an acorn and wait."

One evening I heard a pitiful little cry outside my window. Standing among the roses was a beat-up, scrawny kitten, so thin and hungry it could hardly stand up. I ran to the door but the cat darted away. I had no meat in the house, let alone cat food, so I filled a plate with brown rice and tofu and put it outside the door. The kitty came warily out of the bushes, sniffing the food, and then jumped at it as if he were pouncing on his prey. He choked the food down as fast as he could. I called him inside, but he turned and ran.

Next morning he was back crying at the window. I warmed some soy milk, put it out the door, and let him take a drink. He shuddered while he ate this ungodly concoction, but came back for more. I moved the bowl inside the door. The cat followed cautiously. This went on for three days until he would freely enter the door whenever he wished. He became a vegetarian and ate what I ate, except for granola. He would even eat granola if I let it soak long enough in milk. Sometimes he couldn't take vegetarianism any longer and made brief forays into the wild to get a little mouse on the hoof.

Clearly this was a wild cat that had never lived indoors. He liked to be outside all the time hunting, chasing butterflies in the roses, or swatting petals off Mr. Lincoln. He liked to sleep indoors most nights, but when the sun started to come up, he would start kneading my face with his paws. If I didn't wake up quick enough, he started easing out his razor-sharp claws to make sure I got the message. When I opened my eyes, he would start his turbo-charged purring. His entire body would shake as though propelled by some noisy, out-of-whack, electric motor.

He had no one and neither did I. We needed each other and we became best friends.

I called him Ha Ha because he had a devilish sense of humor. At night, he would climb up onto the stove, then the top of the refrigerator, and wait quietly in the dark until I came into the kitchen. Then he would jump from the refrigerator onto my back with his claws out, hissing loudly as he flew. He would scare me out of my wits, tear my shirt, and scratch my back with one bold move. Then he would run away and hide, making weird little noises that I imagined to be laughter. So I called him Ha Ha.

I made a cloth pouch with a strap that I could sling across my shoulder. Ha Ha would ride in the pocket. I borrowed a bicycle and pedaled around Santa Barbara with Ha Ha looking out of his pouch.

I took him to the library with me, and he would never try to get out. It was at the library that I found a copy of *Authentic American Cowboys and Their Songs*. It was a collection of old 78s from the 1920s reissued in a single album. I checked it out hoping that somehow I could get a record player. That weekend my employers had a yard sale and among the junk I found a funky little player with two speeds, too fast and too slow.

With that three-dollar machine I listened to *Authentic Cowboy Songs* and heard music that really moved me. These were not dime-store movie cowboys, but rough-and-tumble men who herded cattle on the open range around the turn of the century. They had names like Jules Verne Allen, Haywire Mac McClintook, and Carl Sprague. Their voices were real, raw and unself-conscious. I had never done any singing before in my life, but these guys spoke to me. The sound of their rough voices gave me the confidence to sing. I felt like a cowboy: no real home, out there alone, riding herd over several hundred head of roses, and relating only to my horse, which happened to be a cat. These old-time cowboy songs were basic and raw, which is the way I felt all the time. They were about being alone.

At night I would practice these songs, and Ha Ha would listen. He would stretch out on the bed and listen nonchalantly, one eye open, never criticizing or complaining about my being out of tune. Often he would climb on my shoulders and curl up around my neck for a better view. Maybe he just liked to be close to the source of the sound, or maybe it was just his subtle way of encouraging me. His warmth and mighty purring would loosen up any reservations I had about singing.

We especially liked "The Old Chilsom Trail" by Carl Sprague. It was a lively number that caused Ha Ha to stand on my shoulders and pace. It got to be a little game: I would sing and try to toss him off by moving my shoulders up and down and he would try to stay on. I imagined he was dancing to the music.

On the liner notes of the record it said that Carl Sprague of Bryan, Texas, was the first cowboy singer ever to make a record, back in 1927. It also noted that he was the only one of the singers still living. I began to think how great it would be to meet him and learn to play these songs and harmonica tunes directly from the source. It became my daydream to find this old cowboy singer and see if he would teach me.

One night I was cooking dinner when Ha Ha walked slowly into the kitchen. His eyes looked glassy. I said, "Ha Ha, are you feeling OK?" Just then his legs stiffened and his ears went back, as though he were feeling an electric shock. It passed and he leaned against the wall. I turned to him, "Ha Ha, what's wrong?" His legs stiffened again, his fur stood straight up, his eyes were wide, his teeth bared, his ears flat against his head. A tremendous surge of energy went through his body, as though every cell were exploding. He looked like he was traveling through space at a million miles an hour. Within seconds he slumped against the wall and was dead.

I doubled over in sadness and pain and burst out crying. I sat there beside him, until midnight, in shock. I had no one to tell, no one to talk to. . . . My friend was dead.

The next morning I wrapped him in one of the shirts he loved to claw and tied the sleeves around him. I decided to bury him in the rose garden by the door, where he had first come into my life. As I was digging the hole, I realized something was ending. I could no longer stay isolated and alone. It was time to move on. What I wanted to do most was go find Carl Sprague in Texas and see if I could learn a little of what he knew. And as I covered Ha Ha with earth I decided to go back to Texas and patch things up with my parents and seek out that old cowboy singer. I had been sitting on the acorn long enough—it was time to start climbing the branches.

A few days later I closed the door to the apartment for the last time. I said good-bye to my friend buried there, and good-bye to the sweet smell of roses.

David Holt did go to Texas and find the old cowboy singer, Carl Sprague. Sprague taught him to play harmonica and sing such cowboy favorites as "Bury Me Not on the Lone Prairie." Realizing that there were many traditional musicians living in the Blue Ridge Mountains, Holt moved to Asheville, North Carolina, to learn directly from the old-time mountaineers. He has been collecting and performing this music for over twenty-five years. He has hosted traditional music shows for PBS, NPR, and the Nashville Network.

DAVID GUTERSON

On Bookstores

OVER THE past two years, I've had the good fortune to visit dozens and dozens of bookstores and to get a glimpse of how bookstores operate and of their role in the publishing community. The bookselling business, I've come to see, is ceaselessly energized not only by market forces and by the bitter mechanics of competition in the capitalist economy of the late 20th century, but more importantly by *people*, individuals who care about books, who love them deeply for all the right reasons, and who want others to love them too.

It is this love of books that makes a bookstore truly a bookstore, and there is no way this love can be faked, either—it is either inherent in the place or it isn't, and it is only inherent in the place when it is also inherent in the hearts of the people who work there. You can feel this when you walk into certain stores, a quality of spirit, finally, something vaguely at odds with the mercantile essence of the place—that same feeling you get in certain classrooms and libraries that stems from certain teachers and librarians—a quality of love, a sense of reverence, a respect for art and for knowledge and learning, for ideas, poems, stories, novels, and for the human spirit in its grandest forms.

Bookstores at their best have this quality too, and it is precisely this that makes them inviting places, places we gravitate toward in our spare time, full of light and of possibility, less like shopping for something we need and more like a vital interlude of some sort, so that we feel a little thrill of possibility, a quietly animated expectation, whenever we walk through the door. And this is not a function, really, of how or where the books are arranged, or what sort of coffee is served—if any—or of where the magazines are relative to the door, or of the lighting, posters, displays, and so forth—the fashion statements of the clerks on the floor—but finally, for me, something to be noted foremost in the eyes of the people who work in a given bookstore, an honest feeling for the task they are about, an honest love of books generally, and this is irreducible and irreplaceable.

David Guterson, from his acceptance speech upon receiving the American Booksellers Book of the Year Award for Snow Falling on Cedars; *used by permission.*

POET

BY

PETER SÍS

LYNNE REID BANKS

THE JEWEL TREE

THE MAIN reason why Freda Martin liked her life was, of course, because she spent a fair proportion of it doing the thing she loved best—painting pictures. Another reason was because she felt confident that she was in command of her own destiny.

Not for her the throw-away lines she heard continually from the women around her: "Well, I mean, life takes hold of you, doesn't it? It's not up to you what happens;" or, "Along came Kevin/John/Barry/Dave, and next thing I knew we were married." In these apparently casual remarks, Freda heard, not without a repressed feeling of impatience, the faint, feeble cries of people being borne away on a swift-running tide in little, careless craft—not just out of control, but not even stopping to consider that if they jumped out and swam for the shore, they could probably walk, at their own pace, to some destination of their own choice.

Freda had swum to shore in her early twenties, leaving the frail coracle of an ordinary woman's destiny to drift where it would. She was different. She was an artist. Men didn't strike her as being up to much, in the main, though there were a few who made nice friends. As for marriage, she was already aware that that was a lottery. It was one, she decided, on which she was not prepared to risk any spiritual currency.

She watched her contemporaries pairing off, setting up house, producing families, and in general dwindling into wives. She felt no envy. Why should she? She was fortunate. Her parents—missionaries both, with whom her contact had always been fleeting and superficial—succumbed to a tropical epidemic and bequeathed her a house in a London suburb. She converted most of the first floor into a large studio with a north-facing window. One little bedroom, a shower, a kitchenette—that was all she needed. The rest remained as her parents had left it when they went abroad in 1945. She seldom entered the downstairs rooms, heavily curtained and crowded with frowsty mahogany.

Though she was well trained and talented, she didn't deceive herself. Very few earn a living by art. So she sought, and found, a bread-and-butter job in a fashionable fabrics shop owned by a natty little East Ender who had risen in the trade. Her task was to dress the windows and display the goods. For this she did not have to work nine to five like the rest of the staff; nor did she have to dress smartly. A clean blouse in place of her customary painting smock was good enough. The bright colours and varied textures of the fabrics pleased her as much as any could which did not flow from tube to brush to canvas.

The girls in the shop thought her eccentric. So did her friends, who, in the way of the married towards the determinedly single, gradually fell away. "You think yourself well out of this," said one, up to her eyes in nappies and howling toddlers. "All right at thirty. What about when you're forty? Fifty? *Sixty?*" she had added viciously, stung perhaps by Freda's impervious smile.

And men, in their crass way, said worse.

"Can paintings love you and take care of you? Can a picture give you kids? Oh, sure we can go on being friends, but I shall marry someone else. *I* don't intend to spend life alone even if you do."

They didn't go on being friends. They fell away too, into their own paired prefabricated lives. Freda didn't mind. She would climb the stairs to her studio with its solid, multi-coloured easel, its old table cluttered with squashed tubes and jam jars bristling with brushes, and canvasses—stacks of them. White. Stretched. Virginal. "Ah ha!" she thought with a sort of triumph. "Like me!" And she covered them with landscapes and still lifes of a power and pleasingness which she knew increased year by year. It was her chosen portion, and it was enough.

She had a connection with a local gallery that gave her an exhibition every couple of years. The man who ran it, Dennis, was an old, close friend. *He* had never spoilt things by wanting to marry her and tie her down to domesticity. He would walk in without glancing at her cluttered rooms or uncarpeted stairs, the dust on the ledges or the paint smudges on the walls, and follow her to the quiet centre of her world, the small area around her easel. He would clear the rubbish off a hard kitchen chair and sit on it and drink coffee from a chipped mug while she set her latest pictures on the easel for him one by one, and he would tell her, with honesty, affection, and insight, what he thought.

"Nice, Freda! Oh, yes. Love that. Very evocative, that copse. You seem to have got the whole of autumn into it, somehow." And in the end he would knock out his pipe and ask, "When are you going to do the big one for me?"

But Freda didn't feel she had it in her to do a big one.

"I'm a small woman," she would say. "Anything more than three by two would be out of scale with me."

"Trouble with exhibiting Freda Martin," Dennis would grumble, "is I always have to break up my wall." He had a big wall in his gallery facing the door which he liked to occupy with some large and striking work.

But he never gave up on her, even when the exhibitions only sold a quarter, or less, of her paintings.

"Hard times," he would say. "People want bread before circuses."

She never failed to rise to this bait.

"Bread! Circuses! First of all, art is not to be compared to the tawdry, crowd-pleasing vulgarity of a circus. And as for bread, by which I suppose you mean the basic necessities of life, if times are so hard why are all the fancy-goods shops like the one I work for doing so well? Bread, indeed! That'll be the day, when the poor downtrodden workers have to choose between culture and crusts!"

Dennis would give an exaggerated shudder. "When that happens, my dear, you and I will starve together, while the bakers grow fat." The notion of a big bollard of a man like Dennis starving was so absurd that it comforted Freda through thin times when there was a dearth of buyers. The paintings that didn't sell piled up in her house, or she donated them to good causes. The fabric shop gave her enough to live on and buy materials to paint. And the years passed and she was happy and satisfied.

And then the bottom fell out.

One fine spring day, Dennis came to inspect her latest productions with a view to a new exhibition. He sat in his usual chair, wreathed in pipe smoke, while she stood the paintings before him; but instead of his normal flow of appreciation, he merely grunted noncommittally at each one. Freda began to feel a prickling of unease up her spine.

"That's the lot," she said at last, lifting the last landscape off the easel—and waited. She had never had to wait like that before, and it made her feel, quite suddenly, almost sick with suspense.

"Freda," said Dennis rather peevishly after what seemed an hour of cogitation, "they're all the same."

She felt quite blank. No anger or hurt yet. Just bewilderment.

"The same? What do you mean? Every one is completely—"

"I don't mean the same as each other," Dennis said, flapping his hand like a walrus. "I mean the same as last year and the year before."

Now Freda felt outrage creeping in on her. "You mean you see no development," she said coldly.

"Now Freda, my dear, don't take that tone. I see an improvement. In technique. But development? Well, frankly—no."

He stood up and came to where she was standing by the easel. If he noticed her stiff face and apprehensive eyes, he deliberately ignored them. He picked up one of her recent works and stood it up again. She was seized by an idiotic desire to snatch it back and hide it from that bland, critical gaze.

"A typical Martin landscape," he mused. "Now, a recognisable style is a good thing, clients like it. But, when the style gets stereotyped . . ."

"Stereotyped!"

"Look here," he said, pointing with his pipe stem. "That row of trees—the colour range—umbers, rusts, that touch of white. . . . And the skies, the windy look. Brilliantly executed, I grant you, but—typical. Typically *you*, Freda. I've seen that wispy cirrus blowing about the tops of your canvasses for ten years now—or is it fifteen? Yes, yes, I know what you're going to say—"

"I'll bet you don't!" Freda all but exploded, but Dennis pressed on like a large, relentless bulldozer; she had the sensation of being shoved steadily backwards prior to being shovelled up and dumped.

"—The still lifes. No cirrus in *them*, sure enough. But the overall designs—that oft-repeated triangle with the vase or bottle at the apex and the fruit huddled at the base . . . the classic gleam on the blade of that damn' cheese knife . . . that—I must say it, Freda—that *inevitable* Conference pear, like the leaning Tower of Pisa, just off centre—"

"Get out!" screamed Freda.

Dennis, her oldest, truest, most fatally honest friend, stared at her in astonishment—mingled, she could see, with pained disapproval. Freda, both hands pressed to her breast through her faded fisherman's smock, her face red and her eyes wild, stared back, defiance and outrage nakedly displayed.

"My dear," said Dennis at last slowly, in a tone she'd never heard before. "I've hurt you. Believe me, I had no such intention. An artist, though, Freda, must be able to stand up to criticism. Perhaps," he said, half to himself, "I've featherbedded you too much. A safe outlet through my gallery—financial security—a certain number of faithful buyers. . . . That's the way to stagnation."

Freda stood speechless. If he had attacked her physically she could not have been more shocked, more wounded.

"I think what I'd better say," Dennis continued, "is that until you move out of this phase of your artistic development, our partnership is—not ended, of course not, but—shall we say, in abeyance?"

He delivered this *coup de grace* quietly, then picked up his coat, smiled at her his characteristic lopsided smile, and shambled away, leaving her devastated among the canvasses.

For three months after that she didn't touch a brush, didn't look at a palette. She expelled from her mind every tentative would-be-painted image that crept into it.

She had to fill her painting time, so she took on extra work at the shop. She changed the window display every week instead of every fortnight, filled in when a salesgirl left—and suddenly, without having wanted it, found herself noticed.

"You're quite a little bundle of dynamite these days, Freda," her boss remarked in his waggish fashion. "If you don't want to find yourself running the whole *gesheft* you'd better slow down."

She didn't. She couldn't. She worked later and later to avoid going home. The studio which had been the centre of her life became a purgatory. When she had to be in the house, she stayed downstairs. She'd never spent a lot of time down there, nor noticed the mounting chaos of the lower rooms, which she'd used mainly for storage. Now, grudgingly, she began to make them habitable.

She started tidying simply because she couldn't bear the piles of unbought canvasses lying everywhere. What she had regarded before as simply the natural surplus of her profession, she now saw as rejects. At first she tried to look at each one objectively before carrying it up to the attic to hide it away; but Dennis had spoilt them all for her. If there were a wisp of cloud above a landscape, a shade of russet in the foliage, or—worst of all, somehow—a pear lurking in a still life, she would want to hurl the painting straight through the nearest window. If there were none, she would have to subdue an urge to rush round to the gallery, waving the canvas and crying, like a child, "You see? No clouds! No wind! No cheese knife!"

Yet she couldn't do anything except carry them up—what an awful lot there seemed to be, dozens, scores, all unwanted (boring . . . typical . . . *stagnant* . . .), wrap them carelessly in polythene bags, and shove them into the musty space under the eaves. Then she hurried down again. Not to idleness—that would have been unbearable. She bought a different kind of brush and painted the living room. She even borrowed a Hoover.

Dennis phoned.

"How's it going?" he asked as he always did. As if nothing had changed.

"How's what going?"

"The work, of course."

"Oh, fine," she said brightly. "I've been promoted."

After a puzzled silence, he asked, "To what? What do you mean?"

"In my job. At the shop. I've been made chief buyer."

"Who cares about that?" Dennis asked irritably. "That's not what I call your work, and you know it."

"It's all the work I'm doing at the moment, and it's keeping me fully occupied," she retorted, and put down the receiver.

Despite all the energy she was burning up, both in work and in emotion, she wasn't sleeping well. She'd used to sleep so soundly that on one occasion, a burglar had done the whole house over without causing her to stir. Now she began lying awake, or waking up in the night, filled with an indefinable restlessness and inner pain like heartburn. She swallowed various sorts of tablets and even took to drinking hot whisky toddies last thing, but nothing helped.

And something else unlooked-for happened. She began to mind living alone.

She discovered that it was unpleasant to wake in the night and have no one to talk to, or to come home from a hard, unsatisfying day's work and wander about an empty house. Solitary meals—a thing she'd never minded as long as her imagination had been seething with things she wanted to paint—began to depress her to a point where she almost stopped eating altogether.

She lost weight. At first she told herself she could well spare it; her habitual loose-fitting smocks and jeans had concealed a certain dumpiness for some years past. Now the boss at the fabrics shop began to say things like, "Look at our Freda! Getting ever so svelte. Why don't you treat yourself to a few new rags, darling? I can get them for you at trade discount." Now she was his buyer, he evidently wanted her to smarten up a bit. Once she would have laughed at the idea. Now she shrugged and let him press on her a couple of suits and dresses. Everyone at work agreed she looked a new woman in them. Freda secretly agreed—a new woman whom she herself neither recognised nor liked.

A month later, the new 'rags' began to hang on her.

"Don't overdo that diet, darling, will you?" said the boss with a note of concern.

"We'll be able to use you as a curtain rail soon."

At this Freda felt a totally unaccustomed pricking behind her eyelids. She begged off early and went to a film. It was full of blood and violence. To her surprise, she liked it. When she got home, she drank a whisky without the toddy and went straight to bed.

She woke up in the night. She'd been dreaming of Dennis. It was a very nasty sort of dream—all her paintbrushes had turned out to have little stilettos embedded in their handles and she had stood Dennis up against the easel, like the passive partner in a knife-throwing act, and stuck them into him one by one. Blood oozed out in shades of umber and rust, with touches of white. . . . She awoke crying in great raw sobs, and for the first time in her adult life, looked down into a black abyss of loneliness.

She couldn't lie still. Without thinking what she was doing, still half in her nightmare, she climbed out of bed and into her old painting clothes. The feel of the smock dropping over her head, heavy and warm, with its stiff familiar patches of paint, stirred something inside her. She glanced into her mirror; by the sulphurous streetlight she saw a thin, haggard distortion of her old self—the self which had stood alone, needing no one's company or comfort. That person she had been happy to be, she realised suddenly, had been held upright by the spinal column of talent.

She had another whisky to warm her and then slowly made her way upstairs to the studio. She didn't want to go up there, but she seemed to have no other recourse.

The whole room felt cold with neglect. As she shrinkingly switched on the light, she saw dust everywhere—even cobwebs. The sight horrified her, as if she had shut up something alive and left it to die. This was her place, and she had abandoned it. She felt like weeping with something like remorse as she stood staring round.

She had certainly had no intention of painting when she wandered up here in search of some unspecified comfort of the only kind she knew. Now she found herself wiping the easel clean, setting up a canvas, running her fingers ruefully over the hardened ridges of the paints which had been ready, rich and moist, on her palette when Dennis had frozen all creativity in her with his callousness. She scraped them off with a knife, and wiped the wood with a cloth soaked in turps. Then she looked at the canvas.

She had never worked from reality, only from imagination or memory. Usually when she stared at a blank canvas ghosts of shapes and colours would appear. Now nothing happened—nothing came.

It was the light, perhaps. She only ever painted by daylight. The unshaded bulb glared at a deadening angle on the canvas, throwing weird shadows. She looked round despairingly. She longed to paint again, but the studio had withdrawn its magic. She had left it alone too long—now it was punishing her.

She sat where Dennis had sat, holding her palette and her brushes, staring blankly not at the canvas but at the white wall opposite the big north-facing window. Her wretchedness sank in her like a pit. After a while she got up numbly and switched off that glaring light and then went back and sat in the dark.

Alone. Without joy, without companionship, without the satisfaction of a *métier*—for the rest of her life. She stared that prospect in the face for hours.

Imperceptibly the wall turned from deepest grey to paler. The dawn chorus began. Freda didn't hear it. She stared at the wall, watching its slow return to full visibility. And suddenly she moved—a sharp forward tilt of her body.

Something had appeared on the wall.

It was a tree. Not like those she normally painted. It was half way between an oak and an olive. It grew out of a fantastic landscape, like nothing she had ever seen or imagined. There were flowers there, and strange cactus plants, and exotic fauna. As she gazed, willing her mind's eye to elaborate, she saw a beautiful chestnut horse, diminished by the huge growths, standing calmly beneath the tree.

And from the tree itself hung fruits that were not fruits. She couldn't make out what they were. She knew she would have to paint them to find out.

The light strengthened.

Freda stood up. Swift and sure, she moved to the table where her paint tubes lay in an orderly row. She unscrewed their tops. In the past she had stuck to three or four colours at a time—she was parsimonious with paint—and usually all in the same range ("Yes, Dennis, yes, you were right!"). Now she took the smaller tubes too, the ones she normally reserved for the odd touch—cobalt, vermilion, chrome, ultramarine. Her palette, habitually so staid in its garb of browns and dark greens, burst out like a rainbow in a child's painting-book.

She ignored the easel and the canvas, her eyes fixed on the wall. The day was fully alive, the light too had a life of its own—it was not the steady, reliable north light she was used to; at this hour the sun struck that wall and danced on it. The ghosts of the strange fruits dazzled her inner eye. She approached the wall delicately, almost on tiptoe.

She didn't go to work for a week. She phoned the shop and said she was ill. The precise opposite was the truth. Between bouts of painting she would run downstairs and ransack her store-cupboard for things to eat and drink. She slept—when she slept—like the dead, waking at dawn, showering tinglingly, and rushing back upstairs in time to catch that magic dancing hour before the light settled. She had never felt fitter in her life.

At the end of the week she phoned Dennis.

"I want to show you something."

"Rather pushed just now—big exhibition coming off—"

"Right, don't bother." She hung up.

He was at the door ten minutes later.

"Well? Let's see?"

She led him up and opened the door for him. His eyes went to the easel, but only for a second. He didn't sit down this time. He stood in the doorway and gazed.

"Who did it?" he asked at last.

"Who do you think?"

"Not you!" he said. She didn't answer. He looked at her slowly, as if reluctant to look away from the wall. "I can't believe it!"

"What do you think of it?"

"It's incredible, Freda. Incredible. A complete departure. What happened?"

"I—" But no. It was not his business. She couldn't explain anyway. She couldn't say, I was afraid. I was hurt. I didn't want to go on living. And out of that, mystery and fantasy and a new world were born.

He was closer now, peering at details. "How did you learn to paint horses?"

"I learnt at art school. I just never wanted to paint a horse before."

"You know what a horse always stands for, in art as in dreams, don't you?" he asked, throwing her a mischievous look.

"Sex? Yes, I know."

"But the tree!" he moved closer. "A tree that grows jewels! What are we to make of that?"

"Whatever you want."

"It could have been a load of kitsch. But it's magnificent. And—Freda—furthermore, it's *big*."

"Yes," she said shortly. "Too bad it's a mural and can't be moved."

"Did you do it that way to get back at me?"

"Not consciously."

"I've got to have it on *my* wall, you know that."

"How?"

"You'll have to copy it. Can you?"

"No. But I can do others like it."

He beamed. "I'll stand you the big canvasses. Advance on commission! They'll sell. Bet you. You'll move on. . . . My little pad won't hold you for long if you keep on like this."

He looked forlorn, but then he brightened up.

"But you'll let me give the first exhibition of the new stuff?"

"If you give me lots of encouragement," she said, smiling, it seemed, for the first time in moons.

He was looking at her, frowning slightly.

"What's happened to you?" he asked. "You've changed as much as your work. You're looking very nice."

"You're too kind," she said, but sarcasm was lost on him.

"How long have we known each other? Fifteen years? And I've never once taken you out to dinner."

"Why on earth should you?"

"Well, now I'm going to. When are you free?"

But she'd stopped listening. She was staring with narrowed eyes at the empty easel, imagining the huge canvas that would soon stand on it. White. Stretched. Virginal . . .

"Ah ha! Like me," she said.

"What?"

She turned to him. "Dennis, would you mind going now and buying the first of those canvasses you promised? I want to start work on the big one."

She was at the table with her back to him, sorting paints, when he left. He paused at the door to give a very audible sigh. But she didn't seem to hear.

BARRY LOPEZ

My Hands

MY HANDS were born breech in the winter of 1945, two hours before sunrise. Sitting with them today, two thousand miles and more from that spot, turning each one slowly in bright sunshine, watching the incisive light raise short, pale lines from old cuts, and seeing the odd cant of the left ring finger, I know they have a history, though I cannot remember where it starts. As they began, they gripped whatever might hold me upright, surely caressed and kneaded my mother's breasts, yanked at the restrictions of pajamas. And then they learned to work buttons, to tie shoelaces and lift the milk glass, to work together.

The pressure and friction of a pencil as I labored down the spelling of words right-handed raised the oldest permanent mark, a callus on the third joint of the middle finger. I remember no trying accident to either hand in these early years, though there must have been glass cuts, thorn punctures, spider bites, nails torn to the cuticle, scrapes from bicycle falls, pin blisters from kitchen grease, splinters, nails blackened from door pinches, pain lingering from having all four fingers forced backward at once, and the first true weariness, coming from work with lumber and stones; with tools made for larger hands.

It is from these first years, 5 and 6 and 7, that I am able to remember so well, or perhaps the hands themselves remember, a great range of texture—the subtle corrugation of cardboard boxes, the slickness of the oilcloth on the kitchen table, the shuddering bend of a horse's short-haired belly, the even give in warm wax, the raised oak grain in my school-desk top, the fuzziness of dead bumblebees, the coarseness of sheaves immediate to the polished silk of unhusked corn, the burnish of rake handles and bucket bails, the rigidness of the bony crest rising beneath the skin of a dog's head, the tackiness of flypaper, the sharpness of saws and ice picks.

It is impossible to determine where in any such specific memory, of course, texture gives way to heft, to shape, to temperature. The coolness of a camellia petal seems inseparable from that texture, warmth from the velvet rub of a horse's nose, heft from a brick's dry burr. And what can be said, as the hand recalls the earliest touch and exploration, of how texture changes with depth? Not alone the press of the palm on a dog's head or fingers boring to the roots of wool on a sheep's flank, but of, say, what happens with an orange: The hands work in concert to disassemble the fruit, running a thumb over the beaded surface of the skin, plying the soft white flay of the interior, the stringnet of fiber clinging to the translucent skin cases, dividing the yielding grain of the flesh beneath, with its hard, wrinkled seeds. And, further, how is one to separate these textures from a memory of the burst of fragrance as the skin is torn, or from the sound of the sections being parted—to say nothing of the taste, juice dripping from the chin, or the urge to devour, then, even the astringent skin, all initiated by the curiosity of the hands?

Looking back, it's easy to see that the education of the hands (and so the person) begins like a language: a gathering of simple words, the assembly of simple sentences, all this leading eventually to the forging of instructive metaphors. Afterward nothing can truly be separated, to stand alone in the hands' tactile memory. Taking the lay of the dog's fur, the slow petting of the loved dog is the increasingly complicated heart speaking with the hand.

Still, because of an occasional, surprising flair of the hands, the insistence of their scarred surfaces, it is possible for me to sustain the illusion that they have a history independent of the mind's perception, the heart's passion; a history of gathering what appeals, of expressing exasperation with their own stupidity, of faith in the accrual of brute work. If my hands began to explore complex knowledge by seeking and sorting texture—I am compelled to believe this—then the first names my memory truly embraced came from the hands' differentiating among fruits and woven fabrics.

Growing on farms and in orchards and truck gardens around our home in rural California was a chaos of fruit: navel and Valencia oranges, tangerines, red and yellow grapefruit, pomegranates, lemons, pomelos, greengage and Damson plums, freestone and cling peaches, apricots, figs, tangelos, Concord and muscadine grapes. Nectarines, Crenshaw, casaba, and honeydew melons, watermelons, and cantaloupes. My boyish hands knew the planting, the pruning, the picking, and the packing of some of these fruits, the force and the touch required. I sought them all out for the resilience of their ripeness and knew the different sensation of each— pips, radius, cleavage. I ate even tart pomegranates with ardor, from melons I dug gobs of succulent meat with mouth and fingers. Slicing open a cantaloupe or a melon with a knife, I would hesitate always at the sight of the cleft fistula of seeds. It unsettled me, as if it were the fruit's knowing brain.

The fabrics were my mother's. They were stacked in bolts catawampus on open shelves and in a closet in a room in our small house where she both slept and sewed, where she laid out skirts, suits, and dresses for her customers. Lawn, organdy, batiste, and other fine cottons; cambric and gingham; silks—moiré, crepe de Chine, taffeta; handkerchief and other weights of linen; light wools like gabardine; silk and cotton damasks; silk and rayon satins; cotton and wool twills; velvet; netted cloths like tulle. These fabrics differed not only in their texture and weave, in the fineness of their threads, but in the way they passed or reflected light, in their drape, and, most obviously from a distance, in their color and pattern.

I handled these fabrics as though they were animal skins, opening out bolts on the couch when Mother was working, holding them against the window light, raking them with my nails, crumpling them in my fist, then furling them as neatly as I could. Decades later, reading "samite of Ethnise" and "uncut rolls of brocade of Tabronit" in a paperback translation of Wolfram von Eschenback's *Parzival*, I watched my free hand rise up to welcome the touch of these cloths.

It embarrassed and confounded me that other boys knew so little of cloth, and mocked the knowledge; but growing up with orchards and groves and vine fields, we shared a conventional, peculiar intimacy with fruit. We pelted one another with rotten plums and the green husks of walnuts. We flipped gourds and rolled melons into the paths of oncoming, unsuspecting cars. This prank of the hand—throwing, rolling, flipping—meant nothing without the close companionship of the eye. The eye measured the distance, the crossing or closing speed of the object, and then the hand—the wrist snapping, the fingers' tips guiding to the last—decided upon a single trajectory, measured force, and then a rotten plum hit someone square in the back or sailed wide, or the melon exploded beneath a tire or rolled cleanly to the far side of the road. And we clapped in glee and wiped our hands on our pants.

In these early years—8 and 9 and 10—the hands became attuned to each other. They began to slide the hafts of pitchforks and pry bars smoothly, to be more aware of each other's placement for leverage and of the slight difference in strength. It would be three or four more years before, playing the infield in baseball, I would sense the spatial and temporal depth of awareness my hands had of each other, would feel, short-hopping a sharp grounder blind in front of third base, flicking the ball from gloved-left to bare-right hand, making the cross-body throw, that ballet-ic poise of the still fingers after the release, would sense how mindless the beauty of it was.

I do not remember the ascendancy of the right hand. It was the one I was forced to write with, though by that time the right hand could already have asserted itself, reaching always first for a hammer or a peach. As I began to be judged according to the performance of my right hand alone—how well it imitated the Palmer cursive, how legibly it totaled mathematical figures—perhaps here is where the hands first realized how complicated their relationship would become. I remember a furious nun grabbing my 6-year-old hands in prayer and wrenching the right thumb from under the left. Right over left, she insisted. *Right over left.* Right over left in praying to God.

In these early years my hands were frequently folded in prayer. They, too, collected chickens' eggs, contended with the neat assembly of plastic fighter planes, picked knots from bale twine, clapped chalkboard erasers, took trout off baited hooks, and troweled flower beds. They harbored and applauded homing pigeons. When I was 11, my mother married again and we moved east to a large city. The same hands took on new city tasks, struggled more often with coins and with tying the Windsor knot. Also, now, they pursued a more diligent and precise combing of my hair. And were in anxious anticipation of touching a girl. And that caress having been given, one hand confirmed the memory later with the other in exuberant disbelief. They overhauled and pulled at each other like puppies.

I remember from these years—14 and 15 and 16—marveling at the dexterity of my hands. In games of catch, one hand tipped the falling ball to the other, to be seized firmly in the same instant the body crashed to the ground. Or the hands changed effortlessly on the dribble at the start of a fast break in basketball. I remember disassembling, cleaning, and reassembling a two-barrel carburetor, knowing the memory of where the tiny parts fit was within my hands. I can recall the baton reversal of a pencil as I wrote then erased, wrote then erased, composing sentences on a sheet of paper. And I remember how the hands, so clever with a ball, so deft with a pair of needle-nose pliers, fumbled attaching a cimbidium orchid so close to a girl's body, so near the mysterious breast.

By now, 16 or so, my hands were as accustomed to books, to magazines, newspapers, and typing paper, as they were to mechanic's tools and baseballs. A blade in my pocketknife was a shape my fingers had experienced years earlier as an ole-ander leaf. The shape of my fountain pen I knew first as a eucalyptus twig, draw-ing make-believe roads in wet ground. As my hands had once strained to bring small bluegills to shore, now they reeled striped bass from the Atlantic's surf. As they had once entwined horses' manes, now they twirled girls' ponytails. I had stripped them in those years of manure, paint, axle grease, animal gore, plaster, soap suds, and machine oil; I had cleaned them of sap and tar and putty, of pond scum and potting soil, of fish scales and grass stains. The gashes and cuts had healed smoothly. They were lithe, strenuous. The unimpeded reach of the fingers away from one another in three planes, their extreme effective span, was a subtle source of confidence and wonder. They showed succinctly the physical intelligence of the body. They expressed so unmistakably the vulnerability in sexual desire. They drew so deliberately the curtains of my privacy.

One July afternoon I stood at an ocean breakwater with a friend, firing stones one after another in long, beautiful arcs a hundred feet to the edge of the water. We threw for accuracy, aiming to hit small breaking waves with cutting *thwips*. My friend tired of the game and lay down on his towel. A few moments later I turned and threw in a single motion just as he leapt to his feet. The stone caught him full in the side of the head. He was in the hospital a month with a fractured skull, unable to speak clearly until he was operated on. The following summer we were playing baseball together again, but I could not throw hard or accurately for months after the accident, and I shied away completely from a growing desire to be a pitcher.

My hands lost innocence or gained humanity that day, as they had another day when I was pulled off my first dog, screaming, my hands grasping feebly in the air, after he'd been run over and killed in the road. Lying awake at night I sometimes remember throwing the near-deadly stone, or smacking a neighbor's cat with my adolescent fist, or heedlessly swinging a 16-gauge shotgun, leading quail—if I hadn't forgotten to switch off the trigger safety, I would have shot an uncle in the head. My hands lay silent at my sides those nights. No memory of their grace or benediction could change their melancholy stillness.

While I was in college I worked two summers at a ranch in Wyoming. My hands got the feel of new tools—foot nips, frog pick, fence pliers, skiving knife. I began to see that the invention, dexterity, and quickness of the hands could take many directions in a man's life; and that a man should be attentive to what his hands loved to do, and so learn not only what he might be good at for a long time but what would make him happy. It pleased me to smooth every wrinkle from a sad-dle blanket before I settled a saddle squarely on a horse's back. And I liked, too, to turn the thin pages of a Latin edition of the *Aeneid* as I slowly accomplished them that first summer, feeling the impression of the type. It was strengthening to work with my hands, with ropes and bridles and hay bales, with double-bitted axes and bow saws, currying horses, scooping grain, adding my hands' oil to wooden door latches in the barn, calming horses at the foot of a loading ramp, adjusting my hat against the sun, buckling my chaps on a frosty morning. I'd watch the same hand lay a book lovingly on a night table and reach for the lamp's pull cord.

I had never learned to type, but by that second summer, at 19, I was writing out the first few stories longhand in pencil. I liked the sound and the sight of the writing going on, the back pressure through my hand. When I had erased and crossed out and rewritten a story all the way through, I would type it out slowly with two or sometimes four fingers, my right thumb on the space bar, as I do to this day. Certain keys and a spot on the space bar are worn through to metal on my typewriters from the oblique angles at which my fingernails strike them.

Had I been able to grasp it during those summers in Wyoming, I might have seen that I couldn't get far from writing stories and physical work, either activity, and remain happy. It proved true that in these two movements my hands found their chief joy, aside from the touching of other human beings. But I could not see it then. My hands only sought out and gave in to the pleasures.

I began to travel extensively while I was in college. Eventually I visited many places, staying with different sorts of people. Most worked some substantial part of the day with their hands. I gravitated toward the company of cowboys and farmers both, to the work of loggers and orchardists, but mostly toward the company of field biologists, college-educated men and women who worked long days open to the weather, studying the lives of wild animals. In their presence, sometimes for weeks at a time, occasionally in stupefying cold or under significant physical strain, I helped wherever I could and wrote in my journal what had happened and, sometimes, what I thought of what had happened. In this way my hands came to know the prick and compression of syringes, the wiring and soldering of radio collars, the arming of anesthetizing guns, the setting of traps and snares, the deployment of otter trawls and plankton tows, the operation of calipers and tripod scales, and the manipulation of various kinds of sieves and packages used to sort and store parts of dead animals, parts created with the use of skinning and butchering knives, with bone saws, teasing needles, tweezers, poultry shears, and hemostatic clamps. My hands were in a dozen kinds of blood, including my own.

Everywhere I journeyed I marveled at the hands of other creatures, at how their palms and digits revealed history, at how well they performed tasks, at the elegant and incontrovertible beauty of their design. I cradled the paws of wolves and polar bears, the hooves of caribou, the forefeet of marine iguanas, the foreflippers of ringed seals and sperm whales, the hands of wallabies, of deer mice. Palpating the tendons, muscles, and bones beneath the skin or fur, I gained a rough understanding of the range of ability, of expression. I could feel where a broken bone had healed and see from superficial scars something of what a life must have been like. Deeper down, with mammals during a necropsy, I could see how blood vessels and layers of fat in a paw or in a flipper were arranged to either rid the creature of its metabolic heat or hoard it. I could see the evidence of arthritis in its phalenges, how that could come to me.

I have never touched a dead human, nor do I wish to. The living hands of another person, however, draw me, as strongly as the eyes. What is their history? What are their emotions? What longing is there? I can follow a cabinetmaker's hands for hours as they verify and detect, shave, fit and rub; or a chef's hands adroitly dicing vegetables or shaping pastry. And who has not known faintness at the sight of a lover's hand? What man has not wished to take up the hands of the woman he loves and pore over them with reverence and curiosity? Who has not in reverie wished to love the lover's hands?

Years after my mother died I visited her oldest living friend. We were doing dishes together and she said, "You have your mother's hands." Was that likeness a shade of love? And if now I say out of respect for my hands I would buy only the finest tools is that, too, not love?

The hands evolve, of course. The creases deepen and the fingers begin to move two or three together at a time. If the hands of a man are put to hard use, the fingers grow blunt. They lose dexterity and the skin calluses over like hide. Hardly a pair of man's hands known to me comes to mind without a broken or dislocated finger, a lost fingertip, a permanently crushed nail. Most women my age carry scars from kitchen and housework, drawer pinches, scalds, knife and glass cuts. We hardly notice them. Sunlight, wind, and weather obscure many of these scars, but I believe the memory of their occurrence never leaves the hands. When I awaken in the night and sense my hands cupped together under the pillow, or when I sit somewhere on a porch, idly watching wind crossing a ripening field, and look down to see my hands nested in my lap as if asleep like two old dogs, it is not hard for me to believe they know. They remember all they have done, all that has happened to them, the ways in which they have been surprised or worked themselves free of desperate trouble, or lost their grip and so caused harm. It's not hard to believe they remember the heads patted, the hands shaken, the apples peeled, the hair braided, the wood split, the gears shifted, the flesh gripped and stroked, and that they convey their feelings to each other.

In recent years my hands have sometimes been very cold for long stretches. It takes little cold now to entirely numb thumbs and forefingers. They cease to speak what they know. When I was 31, I accidentally cut the base of my left thumb, severing nerves, leaving the thumb confused about what was cold, what was hot, and whether or not it was touching something or only thought so. When I was 36, I was helping a friend butcher a whale. We'd been up for many hours under the 24-hour Arctic daylight and were tired. He glanced away and without thinking drove the knife into my wrist. It was a clean wound, easy to close, but with it I lost the nerves to the right thumb. Over the years each thumb has regained some sensitivity, and I believe the hands are more sympathetic to each other because of their similar wounds. The only obvious difference lies with the left hand. A broken metacarpal forced a rerouting of tendons to the middle and ring fingers as it healed and raised a boss of carpal bone tissue on the back of the hand.

At the base of the right thumb is a scar from a climbing accident. On the other thumb, a scar the same length from the jagged edge of a fuel-barrel pump. In strong sunlight, when there is a certain tension in the skin, as I have said, I can stare at my hands for a while, turning them slowly, and remember with them the days, the weather, the people present when some things happened that left scars behind. It bring forth affection for my hands. I recall how, long ago, they learned to differentiate between cotton and raw silk, between husks of the casaba and the honeydew melon, and how they thrilled to the wire bristle of the hog's back, how they clipped the water's surface in swimming-pool fights, how they painstakingly arranged bouquets, how they swung and lifted children. I have begun to wish they would speak to me, tell me stories I have forgotten.

I sit in a chair and look at the scars, the uneven cut of the nails, and reminisce. With them before me I grin as though we held something secret, remembering bad times that left no trace. I cut firewood for my parents once, winter in Alabama, swamping out dry, leafless vines to do so. Not until the next day did I realize the vines were poison ivy. The blisters grew so close and tight my hands straightened like paddles. I had to have them lanced to continue a cross-country trip, to dress and feed myself. And there have been days when my hands stiffened with cold so that I had to quit the work being done, sit it out and whimper with pain as they came slowly back to life. But these moments are inconsequential. I have looked at the pale, wrinkled hands of a drowned boy, and I have seen handless wrists.

If there were a way to speak directly to the hands, to allow them a language of their own, what I would most wish to hear is what they recall of human touch, of the first exploration of the body of another, the caresses, the cradling of breast, of head, of buttock. Does it seem to them as to me that we keep learning, even when the caressed body has been known for years? How do daydreams of an idealized body, one's own or another's, affect the hands' first tentative inquiry? Is the hand purely empirical? Does it apply an imagination? Does it retain a man's shyness, a boy's clumsiness? Do the hands anguish if there is no one to touch?

Tomorrow I shall pull blackberry vines and load a trailer with rotten timber. I will call on my hands to help me dress, to turn the spigot for water for coffee, to pull the newspaper from its tube. I will put my hands in the river and lift water where the sunlight is brightest, a playing with fractured light I never tire of. I will turn the pages of a book about the history of fire in Australia. I will sit at the typewriter, working through a story about a trip to Matagorda Island in Texas. I will ask my hands to undress me. Before I turn out the light, I will fold and set my reading glasses aside. Then I will cup my hands, the left in the right, and slide them under the pillow beneath my head, where they will speculate, as will I, about what we shall handle the next day, and dream, a spooling of their time we might later remember together and I, so slightly separated from them, might recognize.

DOUG
MARLETTE

A Cartoon,
an Apology,
and
an Answer

On June 3 [1994] New York Newsday *printed a Doug Marlette cartoon critical of the Pope. After a storm of protests the paper ran an apology. Responding, Marlette wrote his answer, which* Newsday *published on June 16. Here are the cartoon, the apology, and Marlette's answer.*

AN APOLOGY
MEMO TO READERS

On Friday, *New York Newsday* ran an editorial cartoon in this section which depicted the Pope wearing a button that said "No Women Priests." It bore the caption, "Upon this Rock I will build My Church." While conceived as a critical comment on the recent papal declaration that women can never rise to the priesthood, the cartoon was perceived by many readers to ridicule the Pope and the Roman Catholic church. This was not *New York Newsday*'s intention.

An editorial cartoonist's chief tools are symbols and imagery. With them, an artist telegraphs a message—pointed, funny, or both. It is unfortunate, and we regret, that many readers were given an unintended message in Friday's cartoon.

AN ANSWER TO *NEWSDAY* APOLOGY
BY DOUG MARLETTE

A cartoon I drew recently lit up our switchboard at *Newsday* like the night sky over Baghdad during the Persian Gulf War. It showed the Pope wearing a button that said "No Women Priests." There was an arrow pointing to his forehead and the inscription from Matthew 16:18, "Upon this Rock I will build My Church."

Some *Newsday* readers, seething with outrage, bombarded the publisher, the editors, and me with complaints. "Sacrilege!" they cried. "Anti-Catholic! I'm canceling my subscription." "You're calling the Pope a rockhead!" protested another. One reader accused me of insulting Polish-Americans as well as the Pope. One lady said it was offensive to Catholicism and the Pope, who, as she explained, "may be our highest ranking priest." Obviously this was not a debate conducted on a lofty Jesuitical plane. In fact, I have had more sophisticated theological discussions with snake handlers.

A couple of days later I got a call from *Newsday*'s editorial page editor. "It's been a rough weekend and I have some bad news. We're going to run an apology for the cartoon."

"That is bad news!" I said. It is always bad news when a newspaper apologizes for expressing an opinion—bad news for the First Amendment, bad news for journalism, and bad news for readers. I am paid to express opinions in an interesting, entertaining, and provocative way. *Newsday* apologizing to our readers for that cartoon is a lot like the New York Knicks apologizing to the state of Indiana for Patrick Ewing's series-winning slam dunk against the Pacers.

"Why?" I inquired.

"It was a mistake to run the drawing," he explained.

"A mistake?" I replied. "How can expressing an opinion be a mistake?"

Granted, there is something about good cartoons, the powerful, archaic language of images, that gets under the skin of people in a way that written opinion doesn't. I guess that's why we haven't read any apologies for editorials lately. Or apologies for endless stories in *Newsday* about condoms in schools, Joey and Amy's trysts, the state of John Bobbitt's privates, homosexual marriages, or many other issues offensive to certain Catholic sensibilities.

"You crossed the line," my editor insisted.

"What line?" I asked.

"It was an offense to Catholics," he answered.

"Which Catholics?" I asked. Catholic friends of mine roared with approval at the cartoon. Priests and nuns laughed out loud at the cartoon when it was described to them at a First Communion ceremony the day before.

Newsday's view of Catholicism, I suggested to my editor, is as narrow and congested as the Long Island Expressway. The Catholic Church I know is big enough and secure enough to laugh at this cartoon. The Catholic Church I know and frankly admire is, as its name suggests, "universal" enough and diverse enough to encompass Catholic opinion as wide-ranging and contradictory as that of Cardinal Spellman and Dorothy Day, Mother Teresa and Father Coughlin, Cardinal O'Connor and Pope John 23d, William F. Buckley and Tennessee Williams.

Unfortunately, *Newsday* editors did not hear from Mother Teresa, Pope John 23d, or Tennessee Williams. They heard from furious readers who said such criticism of the Pope is disrespectful. I disagree. I have drawn cartoons on this Pope for years. I have drawn positive cartoons of the Pope, when he was standing courageously toe to toe against Communism's Evil Empire, and I have drawn cartoons critical of him for his position on population control and women priests. It is not disrespectful to satirize and criticize. On the contrary, satire shows true respect because it takes seriously public figures and the stands they take.

For the record, I like this cartoon. I am proud of this cartoon. It is funny and it hit the bull's-eye. I do not apologize for drawing it. It is no more anti-Catholic than the cartoons I have drawn criticizing Farrakhan were anti-Muslim or those criticizing Jerry Falwell were anti-Baptist or those criticizing Menachem Begin were anti-Semitic.

I suspect the reason the howls of protest were so strident was that the cartoon was so on the mark and so . . . well, Catholic. According to polls, over seventy percent of Catholics support the ordination of women. That's certainly more support for women than my own Baptist church can claim. We Baptists, according to polls, view the ordination of women with about as much enthusiasm as the sprinkling of infants. (Of course, Baptists also believe Jesus turned water into Welch's grape juice.) So, my cartoon seems more Catholic to me than Baptist. Although Baptists who number among their faithful President Clinton, Vice President Gore, former *Newsday* publisher Bill Moyers, Jerry Falwell, Jesse Helms, and Dr. Martin Luther King, Jr., can boast almost as lively, conflicted, and variegated a religious tradition as the Holy Roman Church.

Historically, Baptists believe, though this has been obscured by the antics of some of our more visible and mean-spirited brethren like Falwell and Helms, in the importance of individual conscience, what we call "soul freedom," or the competence of the individual before God. This simple belief placed us from the start at the far end of the Protestant Reformation, along with other religious existentialists like the Quakers and Unitarians. We Baptists affirm the efficacy of individual experience, "the priesthood of all believers" as we call it, turning our backs on institutional authorities and mediators of the Holy, like popes and priests, even editors. It should come as no surprise that it was Baptists in Colonial Virginia, no strangers to persecution, who played a key role in giving this nation its First Amendment.

I have drawn controversial political cartoons professionally for twenty-two years, first at *The Charlotte Observer* in my home state of North Carolina and then at *The Atlanta Journal-Constitution*. Drawing opinion in the buckle of the Bible Belt, we got our share of complaints, criticism, petitions urging I be fired, subscription cancellation threats from religious zealots, even death threats. My cartoons were held up on Jim and Tammy Bakker's PTL show and denounced as blasphemous until their televangelism empire was brought crashing down by the confessions of a Long Island woman, Jessica Hahn. Angry viewers would call my newspaper. "You're a tool of Satan," they said. "That's impossible," I replied. "Our personnel department gives tests screening for tools of Satan. Knight-Ridder newspapers have a policy against hiring tools of Satan." They were not amused. Of course, as we have learned this week, religious zealots are not noted for their sense of humor.

One of the cartoons I won the Pulitzer Prize for showed Jerry Falwell, that Pontiff of American right wing Protestantism, as a snake in the PTL Garden of

Eden saying "Jim and Tammy were expelled from the garden and left me in charge." Falwell demanded an apology. His supporters called in shouting "blasphemy!" quoting scripture about the immunity to criticism of God's anointed. I explained that I felt the cartoon was scriptural. There is a rich tradition in the New Testament of referring to religious professionals as snakes. Jesus called the Pharisees, sort of the Moral Majority of his time, a "brood of vipers." John the Baptist and the Old Testament prophets were even less "sensitive."

"THAT'S RIGHT— JIM AND TAMMY WERE EXPELLED FROM PARADISE AND LEFT ME IN CHARGE!"

But in all my years of drawing sacrilege and blasphemy, serving as a tool of Satan and squabbling with editors and publishers over some of those cartoons, not once was a public apology issued for a drawing that ran. Until now.

Since moving to New York five years ago I have run into more censorship and timidity about free speech than I ever encountered in my native South. Surprised? I suspect it is because my editors in Charlotte and Atlanta, though by no means perfect, took these matters more seriously. Because they were Southerners they took their religion more seriously. They certainly took the First Amendment more seriously. Because we Southerners were not raised in a culture suffused with lip service to liberalism and our ideas on race, civil rights, civil liberties were not spoon-fed to us but had to be earned, and for many of us those lessons were costly, our sense of commitment to freedom of expression is less an abstract notion than it seems to be here in the Northeast. Free speech, for us, is not just a liberal whim, a pretty ideal, a cocktail party pronouncement, something we write about in editorials but wuss out on when the heat is on. Perhaps because in the time and place we came up in, during the crucible of the civil rights movement in the South, these ideas lived and breathed and were fought over and acted out in the flesh and blood of our lives. For us, free speech, the right to dissent, freedom of expression, freedom to assemble, the right to vote, these were truly matters of life and death. And their absolute importance to the life and health of a community is not just in our minds now, but in our hearts and in our bones.

Censors no longer come to us in jackboots with torches and clubs and baying dogs and the unbidden knock on the door in the middle of the night. They come to us now in broad daylight, in bow ties and galluses with yellow legal pads and marketing surveys, with focus-group findings and concerns for advertising dollars and bottom lines. They come with degrees from the Columbia School of Journalism and with Pulitzer Prizes to back them up. They are known not for their bravery but for their efficiency. They can only show gallantry when they genuflect and grovel to apologize. They apologize to all Catholics because they believe I offended the Pope. I drew the cartoon because I believe the Pope offended all Catholic women.

In a time when the Church is struggling, attendance is down, financial support is waning, the number of priests entering seminary is dwindling, parochial schools are closing, I expect a certain defensiveness from the faithful. But these readers who hounded *Newsday* for retractions should be ashamed of themselves. Catholics should know better. Theirs is a faith which has suffered historically for its right to express its views freely. From the days when the Church was driven into the catacombs and the crucified bodies of the believers were strewn along the Appian Way to more recent times in places like the Soviet Union, Northern Ireland, and in El Salvador, where priests and nuns have been murdered for preaching the Gospel to the poor, Catholics have suffered when freedom was suppressed. Even in this country not long ago a Catholic couldn't be elected president. There was even a time nuns were pelted with rocks in our nation's capital and forced to hide in attics to celebrate liturgies in secret. It should not be forgotten that Catholics and Jews were not allowed into the Massachusetts Bay Colony until Roger Williams opened Providence Plantation to all those persecuted for their beliefs. Of all people, Catholics should understand the importance of the freedom to express unpopular views without apology.

Since *Newsday* management is mainly a boys club, not famous for its empathy with the concerns and strivings of women, their lackluster support of women priests is not surprising. Their theological naiveté and failure to grasp the richness and complexity of the Catholic faith during their terrible ordeal of trial by phone call is understandable. But what I find most disturbing and beyond comprehension was the lack of fealty of professional newspapermen to the First Amendment.

Isn't this why we have a First Amendment in the first place? So that we don't feel the necessity to apologize for our opinions. We don't need constitutional protection to run boring, inoffensive cartoons. We don't need constitutional protection to make money from advertising. We don't need constitutional protection to tell readers exactly what they want to hear. We need constitutional protection for our right to express unpopular views. The point of opinion pages is to focus attention, to stimulate debate, and to provoke argument. If we can't discuss the great issues of the day on those pages of our newspapers, fearlessly and without apology, where can we discuss them? In the streets with guns?

The Church has always been slow to move on these human matters. After all, it took them until 1993 to forgive Galileo, who whispered in defiance behind the backs of his inquisitors after he was forced to recant the truth, "But still, it moves."

And the same can be said of the Church. "But still, it moves." So I will make a prediction.

There will come a day when a woman stands at the altar of the Holy Roman Church and with all the Catholic world watching, with her fingers blessed by a bishop, she will fully take her place in the Priesthood of Christ and turn bread and wine into the body and blood of our Blessed Redeemer. And it won't be long from now. It may be after the Pope has passed on. But I will bet that most of the people who called in complaining and the editors who apologized for this drawing will live to bear witness to that day. In my opinion, the Pope acted with all the authority of his magesterium, but in his denial of women their right to the priesthood I do not think he acted as Christ would. But after all, I am a Baptist. And we Baptists believe in the priesthood of all believers.

PAUL FLEISCHMAN

BOOK LICE

I was born in a
fine old edition of Schiller

We're book lice
who dwell
in these dusty bookshelves.
Later I lodged in
Scott's works—volume 50

We're book lice
attached
despite contrasting pasts.
One day, while in search of
a new place to eat

We're book lice
who chew
on the bookbinding glue.
We honeymooned in an
old guide book on Greece

While I started life
in a private eye thriller
We're book lice
who dwell
in these dusty bookshelves.

While I passed my youth
in an Agatha Christie
We're book lice
attached
despite contrasting pasts.

He fell down seven shelves,
where we happened to meet
We're book lice
who chew
on the bookbinding glue.

We're book lice
fine mates
despite different tastes.
So we set up our home
inside Roget's Thesaurus

We're book lice
adoring
despite her loud snoring.
And there we've resided,
and there we'll remain,

We're book-loving
book lice

which I'm certain I read
in a book some months back
that opposites
often are known
to attract.

I missed Conan Doyle,
he pined for his Keats
We're book lice
fine mates
despite different tastes.

Not far from my mysteries,
close to his Horace
We're book lice
adoring
despite his loud snoring.

He nearby his Shakespeare,
I near my Spillane
We're book-loving
book lice
plain proof of the fact

that opposites
often are known
to attract.

DAVID NEVIN

DREAM WEST

The following excerpt from my novel Dream West *stands as a celebration of independence, personal strength, and individuality, as a woman of towering inner resources faced with desperate circumstances rises to meet the challenge by turning to writing and publishing.*

Dream West *is an extremely accurate recounting of the lives of John Charles Frémont and Jessie Benton Frémont in the form of a novel. John Charles Frémont was the explorer who mapped and thus opened the Oregon Trail; his reports on the trail were bestsellers that led to the great wagon trains west. He seized California during the Mexican War, opened a river of gold from his Black Drift claim, and lived in a glorious estate, Black Point—now part of the Presidio of San Francisco, a national park. He served in the Senate, ran for President, failed as a Civil War general, and then lost everything in railroad ventures. Gallant to the end, he was a national hero, but a very poor businessman.*

Jessie Benton Frémont, the favorite daughter of Thomas Hart Benton, the great Missouri senator, had passion and political sense to match that of her father. One of the outstanding women of the nineteenth century, she was famous here and abroad, a confidant of presidents and senators and kings. She had a natural talent with words, but what wasn't known until after her husband's death was that, from his notes and descriptions, she had written the exploration reports that had beguiled the nation.

In this excerpt, they now live in a rude little house on Staten Island, which they can barely afford. Frémont is in the West, trying to salvage something from his railroad disasters. Jessie and their unmarried daughter, Lily, are alone; the delicate younger son, Frank, is safely enrolled at West Point. And then a letter comes from the commandant.

My dear General and Mrs. Frémont:

I deeply regret to inform you that the earlier diagnosis has been confirmed. The lesion is not extensive; the condition is mild, but dangerous. Cadet Frémont has been placed on light duty, but I must warn you that the Hudson Valley constitutes a grave danger to anyone with his affliction. I urgently recommend a minimum of six months' residence in a warm, dry climate such as Arizona, which I am reasonably confident would effect a complete cure. The Academy is prepared to grant your son indefinite leave without prejudice. I will wait to hear from you at your earliest—

She lowered the letter, conscious of a flat, rhythmic rapping outside; Mrs. Stanislaus beating her carpet again. Dear, dreamy, musical Frank. She sat very still, her head up, half-hearing the angry *thrap! thrap!* of the carpet beater outside. A warm, dry climate such as Arizona—dear God, *Arizona*, the train fare alone—and he'd have to live when he got there—it would cost a thousand dollars at least. And what if it took longer than the post surgeon predicted?

A thousand dollars.

The government owed them $42,000—at least that—for Black Point and still adamantly refused to pay them for it. A thousand dollars. . . . She had ordered a gown of pale pink moiré from the finest dressmaker in London for her presentation at the Court of St. James; she'd given small fortunes to hospitals during the war and anonymously paid the college tuition for half a hundred impoverished young people; a perfect river of gold had flowed glittering through the baffles at the Black Drift . . . and they couldn't lay hands on a thousand dollars to save the very life of their own son.

She bowed her head, gripping her hands tightly. Careful now. Enough of that.

There was no time now for resentment or remorse; those were luxuries, too, their price too high.

A thousand dollars. There was nothing of value left to sell; they had no credit. She could cook for someone, perhaps, or clean house. Or sew: she was clever with a needle, always had been. But *a thousand dollars*—there was no time to earn that sum. Nancy Davis would give her a thousand dollars if she asked her; so would Hannah Lawrence. But they could never repay it, and you did not use your friends this way. You did not. If only Charles were home! It would be so much easier to bear. But Charles was two thousand miles away, inspecting repair sheds and twenty-seven miles of worthless track somewhere west of Fort Yuma. She would have to meet this alone.

The slap of the carpet-beater seemed to penetrate to the center of her brain, stopping all thought. Desperate for distraction she caught up an old copy of the New York *Ledger*, opened it at random and began reading the first thing she saw. It seemed to be a series of reminiscences about the Duchess of Bedford. Jessie remembered her—a gaunt woman with a horse's face and great yellowed teeth, a deep braying laugh . . . but there wasn't even a hint of that woman here, in this simpering, toffy-nosed creature. How could they print such false trash? This writer had never even laid eyes on the Duchess of Bedford, let alone crossed swords with her over Harriet Martineau's waspish comments on America. Why didn't they assign these pieces to people who had been there, who knew what the grand eminences were really like?

She was on her feet then, staring at the Founder's Medal of the Royal Geographical Society in its case on the far wall, the delicate relief of Apollo striding across the zodiac. . . .

"All right," she said aloud, over the carpet-beater. "Nothing ventured, nothing gained."

An hour later she was on the ferry to Manhattan, wearing her last pair of good black gloves and the coat with the mink collar she rarely wore now because there would never be another.

Robert Bonner came out to her almost as soon as she'd sent in her card. He was Irish, enthusiastic, full of energy. He took her hand and asked after the General and Lily; they all used to ride together along the river north of Tarrytown. Horses were his pleasure, but his joy was the *Ledger*—she thought him the best editor in New York. They chatted a bit and then Jessie said:

"It's occurred to me that some of my experiences, both in Europe and the far West, should have a good deal of interest for your readers."

Nodding, he thrust out his lower lip. "I imagine they would, Mrs. Frémont. Just what sort of article did you have in mind?"

It was the kind of thing she knew how to do, and she did it well: the Duke of Wellington, eighty-four and still the grand old soldier of the century, wandering through the stately rooms at Sion House; the half-naked Indian woman bathing the infant Charley in an earthen bowl deep in the Panama jungles; the Hornitas League claim-jumpers walking toward her in the baked white dust, their rifles glinting; the impeccably aristocratic Comte de la Garde rocking tiny Anne in his arms and crooning a French lullaby; Andrew Jackson's gaunt, leathery face cracking into laughter at her own child's cry, "Hurrah for Old Hickory and the people's bank!"

She stopped, then; she knew when to stop. His eyes were snapping at her, he was biting at the edge of his bright red beard. "It all sounds fascinating, Mrs. Frémont, absolutely fascinating. Of course, *writing* about it is another matter."

"Oh, I've done a great deal of writing."

"Have you?" His pale blue eyes studied her—speculative, a touch patronizing. "I didn't realize that."

"Why yes, you see I—" She broke off. She still could not bring herself to mention the Reports. Not to the world. "Do you know my *Story of the Guard*? It was an account of the gallant war record of the Zagonyi Guards in the West. Ticknor and Fields published it in '63—it went into three editions."

"Yes, of course— I'd forgotten."

"I did much of the biographical material on the General during the presidential campaign in '56. John Bigelow praised my work—I know he'll be happy to corroborate that."

"John liked your work, did he?" Bonner made up his mind then, tapped the desktop. "Well, all right! Why not try a short piece, if you like."

"Good." She took a slow, deep breath. "And now I'd like to talk about payment. What do you pay for such pieces?"

His brows rose, he looked blank with surprise. "Well, of course . . . *if* we liked it. I didn't realize it was a matter of—"

"If you don't like what I've written," she said, "we'll forget the matter. If you do, I will want the professional rate you pay."

"Of course, of course. Well, customarily we, uh, pay a hundred dollars for this kind of article."

"That will be satisfactory."

Still he hung fire, intrigued and amused. "But you'll have to be serious about it, you know."

She raised her head and fixed him with her eyes. "Mr. Bonner," she said, "you have no idea how serious I am." She paused. "I need the money, and I need it at once."

To her surprise he laughed out loud. "That's the best reason anyone ever had for writing anything." He rose and put out his hand. "I'll look forward to reading what you bring us."

At home again she built up the fire, filled the little Georgian inkwell she'd salvaged from the crash, opened her old calf portfolio, fitted a sheet to the blotter backing, and began. She wrote a page, and then another, waiting for that warm, familiar surge of satisfaction. It didn't come. She read over what she'd written and didn't like it very much. She was rusty, that was all; it was years since she'd done any serious writing. She drew a new sheet and started over again. It was better, but not much. Maybe writing was a young person's craft—she was past fifty. Nonsense: look at Cooper, look at Hawthorne . . . look at Dickens and Thackeray.

See the room, *see* Lady Bulwer's full, kindly face, hear her voice. Let it run naturally, easily, as though telling some old, trusted friend. . . .

It grew dark; she lighted the lamp, rebuilt the fire and went back to her desk. Lily came in from work, her face red from the cold, and wanted to talk about the day in her office.

"Be quiet, dear," Jessie said, not unkindly. "I can't talk to you now. I'm writing."

"Writing? Writing what?"

"Never mind now. I have to keep my mind on it."

"But what about supper? Aren't you even going to stop to eat?"

"Later, dear. Perhaps later on."

Lily puttered around in the kitchen, finished up, and went to bed. The raucous neighborhood noises faded, the late silence began to hum. She worked on, sharpening, remembering; holding the moment in her mind's eye, turning it before the mirror of her memory . . . and slowly, stealthily the moments, the sensations came flooding back, flaring like a phosphorescent night tide at Siasconset, teeming with life. Yes, their horizons had shrunk to a row house on Staten Island now; but they had lived the lives of a hundred, a thousand couples; they had laced the country and the hemisphere and half the world, had faced the captains and the kings, found greatness in the humble and pettiness in the great; they'd seen the very world shift on its axis—a continent convulsed with discovery, with migration, with the most terrible of wars. . . .

Charles' life was action: he'd followed it, had done all he could, and more. Now it was up to her. Now the gentler virtues would have to serve. Their lives now were a memory solitaire, where the cards glistened with an occasional tear as she played, and shuffled, and played again, alone in the humming dark. . . .

Bonner was clearly surprised to see her. "Run into trouble?" he asked sympathetically. "I told you it wouldn't be easy."

"It wasn't easy," she said. She opened the bulky package. "But here are ten pieces."

"*Ten pieces?* But it's only been a few weeks, it's only—"

"Sixteen days, to be exact."

He laughed, more in irritation than amusement. "When did you eat? Or sleep?"

"In between drafts." She smiled and handed him the folder. "Tell me what you think of them."

Cornered, he frowned, riffled through the neat manuscript pages. He started to say something, thought better of it, sighed and chose one out of the middle of the sheaf and began to scan the lines. It was one of the lighter pieces, an affectionate cameo of her self-appointed *cavaliere-servente*, the ebullient old Comte de la Garde; an inauspicious start, but there was no help for it. She forced herself to examine various objects in the office. The editor's expression changed as he read on, his irritation faded. A smile appeared, vanished, returned; he began tapping his blue pencil lightly on the desk's edge. He read another, a third. When he was finished he stacked the little block of sheets neatly and squared them against his blotter.

"They're good," he said finally; he shot her an odd glance, almost diffident. "They're very good indeed."

"Thank you."

"Frankly, I'm surprised. Oh, there are a few rough spots, a few places that need polishing here and there. But we can certainly use these, and if the others measure up. . . ."

"Splendid," she said. "Then you wouldn't mind writing me a draft for them while I'm here?"

Robert Bonner stared at her—and burst out laughing again. "I don't see why on earth not, Mrs. Frémont. You've no idea how I have to horsewhip half my writers into producing one story over a month's time. You ought to get a medal for sheer grit."

She smiled. "The check will be sufficient."

He sobered, then. "Mrs. Frémont, I realize this has been a difficult time for you both. I'm really most impressed. Most women would have"—he shrugged eloquently—"well, thrown up their hands and gone under."

"I am not like most women, Mr. Bonner."

"I've just become aware of that!"

"You see—I'm like a deeply built ship. I drive best under a stormy wind."

Outside, on Fourth Avenue, it was snowing hard, whipping under the gaslights, swirling over the bluestone flags like salt; but the slip of paper deep in her purse warmed her to the very tips of her toes. Like Charles on the high plains long ago, sleepless and wary, dogged by doubts, she had hung on and found out what she could do. What she had to do. Not that her talent matched Charles'; she knew her limits. She was not truly creative. Already she realized that everything she wrote had to come from her own experience; she would have to snip the fabric of her life with consummate artistry to realize its full complement of tales; and if her memory faltered, Charles would be there to bring his own rich perceptions to her aid. . . .

She turned, holding the brim of her hat, and waved to a passing hansom. No, nothing she could do would restore their lost position. The success of a Dickens or a Scott was beyond her. They would continue to live on that muddy street above the ferry. But never again would she have to ask Mr. Chaffee to wait for the rent; and that made all the difference in the world.

VIRGINIA HAMILTON

Endings and Beginnings: The Shape of Story

I'M QUITE fond of beginnings, such as waking up in the morning and starting a new day. Occasionally, I awaken from what I term a literary, combination dream. That is, some disguised literary reference combined with a current event. Recently I awoke out of a dream about Maya Angelou as a small child. I wasn't thinking about her, specifically. But she was, of course, some symbol of women writers and, thus, probably represented me. In the dream, she was about toddler age. But she looked the same, had the same laugh and voice as she has today. Yet, she was this very small child in a lovely pink taffeta dress. I had taffeta dresses when I was little. Even when I was big. Taffeta was quite popular into my teen years.

In the dream was my adult self, standing near the child, Angelou, and saying, "Oh, look, there's Ms. Angelou, she's so cute." She was standing in side view, gently stretching her legs and shifting her weight on them, as if trying them out. Next, I saw three numbered lines—1, 2, 3—under each other. And an echoing voice announced, "Maya Angelou takes the silver medal." And then, I woke up. (I had been watching the Olympics the night before.) That's what I mean by a combination dream.

I didn't receive any medals in the dream. It occurred to me that the announcer probably thought I'd had as many as I needed. Then, I was wide awake and wondering, Why didn't she get the gold?

No reason for having Ms. Angelou in my head except that a lot of people real and imagined enter into my nights of dream life. And from her winning the silver medal, not the gold, I thought of the gymnast Shannon Miller, who, after helping her team win a group gold, had difficulty under the pressure of events in an individual competition.

Performing badly, she faced humiliation in front of the world. Then she came back two days later and nailed an individual gold medal. She was able to pull herself together, give herself a new beginning, recreate herself.

It was a pleasure to watch her redefine who she was. There was a real outline for a book there. I watched this kid Shannon start, badly finish, and, finally, find the heart to rethink and reimagine who she was. She redefined herself and started anew. Very, very gutsy—the stuff that fiction is made of. It's always nice when such stuff is real as well. It rather validates the fiction.

Endings, though, are another shade of being. I'm not too fond of them, and I don't dwell on them. But endings make or break a novel. When writing, I allow the ending of a book to creep up on me. I won't write it until everything else is in place and to my mind perfectly executed. I will worry over every part of a book and type all of the changes in good order, save for the ending. All of it will be prepared on neat white sheets of manuscript paper. All finished, all done, except for the ending. Then, I take a deep breath, still holding in all of the tension that has built inside me; and only then do I finally write the close. Dr. Seuss should have written about them—"Endings come, I do not like them, so. I will not follow where they go."

I find starting a new project real enjoyment. A novel, say. It's the beginning of a completely clean slate. It's a new idea of who the author is and what she is capable of. And it's a renewal of language and respect for words that make order out of chaos. No matter what the last project was, a new one gives me a clear chance to be inventive and creative. For rarely does writing work allow acquired knowledge to be applied in the same way more than once. What one learns about writing a single fiction is hopelessly inadequate in writing the next, or any others. Each work is like a new system that must be uncovered. Knowing that I will have to learn to write all over again each time is what startles my mind wide awake through bleary-eyed working mornings.

Writing work is always new. Characters and characterization are different in each book. I've learned to trust my instincts and to have confidence in my thinking—the concept is that if I conceive of some problem or some expression of characters, somewhere within me is the solution or the meaning of the characters.

Between beginning and ending is becoming. Between past and future we stand in tune with memory, evolving in the present time, with recollections of starting and with anticipation or dread, fear, of what's to come and to finish. All of writing involves these aspects of being, becoming, and begone, as does life.

I call forth the child within myself to better understand the adult within. Is the child within a gift to our grown-up selves? The child from my beginning long ago, who sucked in knowledge like a sponge *is* my conscience, my super-ego, and that which holds the standards of family and more symbols of internalized adult behavior. I am the result of my childhood development. All those times alone or listening to favorite adults led me from beginning to becoming.

The language of expression is difficult to learn. We learn it, not because language is greatly complex. We learn words and how to use them—writing, reading—because of the complexity of our thinking. Our thoughts, in turn, grow and change as our needs develop and mature.

I began writing long before I knew what I was doing. And I continued putting words together until I learned or was taught how to structure my thoughts into a coherent form of language. But since the time when I was a child, when I was most impressed by the mystery of sight, sound, and words, writing and making story have been inside me, tapping on my mind-screen for me to let them out.

The myth is that we all have at least one story to tell. People believe that. Someone will say to me, "I know I have a book inside, and someday I'll write it." So many people have expressed that to me. And I think what a person feels or senses is her own expansion, or his own growing. Inside is the person's creation story of beginning and then continuing as he or she shapes the inner self.

In general, each of us changes the shape within and the meaning within by telling ourselves who we are. We keep changing who we are; keep building on and growing ourselves. We learn who we are by living and shaping the story of our lives. And the true story shape is what we believe to be true in ourselves. We change the shape of the story as we define who we are. The story grows and deepens as we do. I believe that's why so many people feel they have at least one story to tell.

I write for what I think are reasonable reasons—to be heard, for enjoyment, to solve problems, because I am masochistic(!). Writing can be so painful at times;

yet, I write to entertain, to be known, and perhaps because I have to. What would I do if I didn't? And I write to see what the story holds, out of curiosity, often finding myself only a few steps ahead of the story in knowing what it is about. I hate writing blind like that. But often, that's the way a book will come. I also must believe I have something particular or important to share with others about the human condition, which I want others to understand as I do. Not necessarily to agree with me, but to listen, to comprehend, and respond to what I believe.

When I write, I don't have real children in mind. I know that sounds odd. But I write about characters, and I think very clearly about them living in some imaginary place.

Ms. Gertrude Stein said, "I am writing for myself and strangers. This is the only way that I can do it. Everybody is a real one to me, everybody is like someone else to me. No one of them that I know can want to know it and so I write for myself and strangers. I want readers so strangers must do it."

She said that while writing *The Making of Americans.*

Writers know as much about the truth or what is best as everyone else. But they like to talk. And by having them talk and write, others among us—readers—are able to collaborate with them in the literary and literacy experience. I think it's true that I write first for myself. But I don't have a clear idea of who out there will be reading what I write. And yet, I don't see whoever they are as strangers.

In my writing, I'm enthusiastic about revealing the voices of young women, particularly those who have difficulty expressing themselves. In a fairly recent novel called *Plain City*, the female protagonist, Buhlaire, has to make choices. These acts of selection are her empowerment and are meant to be seen as part of her gender identity. But the book is really about what happens to a girl character on the way to young adulthood—when she is denied her story of beginning. Thus, she is made static in present time. She cannot move forward, cannot become, because she has no memory about where or how she started. Memory is everything to story.

I begin a book with a character, such as Buhlaire. For years, I thought I began with a display of scene or a vision of movement. It would seem that some story had already begun when I noticed it running in my mind. Usually I heard it coming. But at first I wasn't aware of hearing sound. The scenario was going on. What is this? Then, I'd see someone or hear something on its way to me. And perhaps at that moment, I'd write the someone or something down, questioning what I was seeing second by second—what I smelled in the air or in the field . . . yes, there, I see the field.

I use a computer, which seems to keep up with those questions that occur light-ning-fast. Yet, it took me a long time to understand that what I saw first while writ-ing *always* was the person who then, at once, defined herself, or gave me a clue to the definition of her time, place, and social order. I think it was the editor and publisher Susan Hirschman who first showed me that I started with character. For years I denied it adamantly. But, of course, she was right. It seems such a simple truth now. But for a long time, I couldn't see it.

I believe that to begin a book, it must be about myself; but then, immediately, I let myself go away from it. Writing is all of me, but I disappear into every detail of place and time, character and language. I do so love that about writing, the fact that the writer may disappear. I am very much a hidden person in that way.

There is a metaphor here that describes my way of developing character. The character becomes the trickster and the shape-shifter. The character is free within the story line so that its shape may shift in my mind, which is necessary if it is ever going to stay in the mind of the reader. As author, I may thread from one dimension telling a story about a character's life, within which the character, often a narrator as well, is telling related tales, in order to illuminate further the main thread of the story. The frame technique is something I often use. Its box-like structure, in which reality is tested, is a neat incubator for characters to grow as narrators. The unreliable narrator is always a challenge. I've used this writing device many times in many books from *Arilla Sun Down* to *Plain City*.

Recently, I heard about a writer, a woman, who said her characters lived in this summer house with her. They peopled the hallways, bedrooms, bathrooms, kitchen. She conversed with them. I don't think I'd like it if my characters lived with me. What use would they be? They wouldn't be able to cook or help me make dinner, like a friend or relative might. They might talk about things that related to their circumscribed lives. But writers are very nuts sometimes, or maybe this writer-woman was putting on the interviewer. I've been known to do that. I, too, am in some ways slightly nuts. My daughter occasionally affection-ately e-mails me with the salutation, Dear Mom, you crazy woman. . . .

But I never talk to characters outside of the books where they dwell, for that's where they live, and not with me in my world. I do not write on airplanes, trains, or buses. I do not think about story much outside of where I am writing one. What was it that Ms. Stein also said? "Bear it in your mind my reader, but truly I never feel it that there ever can be for me any such a creature, no it is this scribbled and dirty and lined paper that is really to be to me always my receiver."

Ms. Stein was very aware that to do anything new took courage and strength of purpose, as well as deep desire. And she did her writing where it worked, on the page. I often read from Gertrude Stein's work. She had tremendous word play. We're all familiar with her "a rose is a rose is a rose," but that is only part of an interesting paragraph which goes:

"To suppose, to suppose, suppose a rose is a rose is a rose is a rose. To suppose, we suppose that there arose here and there that here and there there arose an instance of knowing that there are here and there that there are there that they will prepare, that they do care to come again. Are they to come again."

For myself, in my writing, I settle my pages on home, place, the family, and generations. My hope is that my books tell provocative stories, that they will give insights to young people, but not only to young people, but to adults who guide them, and to women, significantly. In writing about female empowerment, one enters the crossroad of cultural learning.

My own beginning story, which I know best, I have watched grow and change, evolve over time as I deepened within. The tale has caused my imagination to leap through my entire career, and it is the story I was born into. My own cultural learning came from true stories and tales of speculation out of the mouths of loved ones. In memory and recollections of family history, ways of being are imbedded—made-up jokes and sayings, ringing styles of speaking from long-gone days and extended families living in close harmony over long times. All very impressive for the child I was, and so, I remember the essence of it all. I have no doubt that much of what I remember is stylized and made emblematic.

There will be a final collection in this series that I have been developing. Two, *Her Stories* and *When Birds Could Talk and Bats Could Sing*, are all finished and published and have become popular with readers. The third collection is again a collaboration between myself and Barry Moser. Collections are interesting. They are not anthologies; they are something else. Collections are derived from a marvelous source of discovery which can be thought of as hundreds of years of a great unpublished book, having innumerable chapters and a seemingly infinite number of stories in all languages from all times—from oral history to the present, and representing all groups and cultures. In *Her Stories* and *Birds and Bats*, I see myself as carrying on an age-old tradition of researching, collecting, and interpreting, and, finally, recasting, refinishing a story, as it were, out of part of the lore of the world.

The Brothers Grimm were interpreters of existing tales in the 1800s with their collections of fairy tales. Preceding them were tales and legends that were translated from the Judeo-German. Some of those stories preceded the Grimm tales by two to three centuries. Called household tales, they were read by generations of people and, especially, by women. The Brothers Grimm insisted that they wrote down faithfully the tales they heard around Germany. But we know they were creative with language.

I try for their remarkable fluidity in my stories, so that the prose language I develop for the recasting of tales brings something of value to readers.

The *Her Stories* collection of nineteen tales demonstrates the broad range of the female African American experience from the Plantation era to the present. By focusing on a single cultural and ethnic group of women, I hoped to reveal a dynamic bond connecting all women. These are generational tales about female children, women, and girls throughout the Plantation era. This is my first all female collection born out of my interest in a certain sense of being female. There is a certain dynamic to working collections, unlike any other in my work. And in *Her Stories*, the female sensibility crosses all barriers of race and culture and economic imperatives. For generations, over centuries, females within individual ethnic groups have shown a profound, creative instinct for story and language as an expression not only of their own oppression but, also, of positive cultural learning.

When Birds Could Talk and Bats Could Sing is illustrated in full watercolor paintings by the master watercolorist, Barry Moser. Moser loved the stories, and I am told that very few of the paintings were ever changed from their precise original renderings. Barry saw what he wanted to do that clearly.

The *Bird* stories are based on African American folktales told in the South during the Plantation era. In the 1880s, Martha Young, a journalist from Alabama, collected them and created many of her own, publishing them in newspapers and then in several books of folktales. Her family had owned slaves. She was three years old at the end of the Civil War, and her family's former slaves became the paid servants of her wealthy household.

Martha Young became an extraordinary collector of black folktales, songs, and sayings and was called a brilliant dialect interpreter. We have no way of knowing how she sounded doing so-called black dialect at the turn of the century. But she was a woman of her time, and the dialect as written is a fractured cross between Gullah speech and an outlandish black language imitation. But she became famous. She performed her stories at Carnegie Hall and was reviewed quite favorably by the *New York Times* and other papers. She collected the black folktales and her own tales, which she created in the African American tradition. She was a contemporary of Joel Chandler Harris; but unlike him and his animal stories, her stories were all about birds and bats. Perhaps that is why they disappeared without a trace until my researcher and I uncovered them. Birds were not as popular as subjects as were the animals, Bruh Rabbit and friends, of the Harris tales.

No longer do we know which bird and bat tales originated with Martha Young and which she had heard from black tellers. I feel, having discovered them, I had a duty to take them back, including hers. All of them are well done, funny, and full of wit. I hear the voices of black tellers in all of them, even in the imitative voice of Martha Young.

Refusing to throw the baby out with the bath water, I have recast the best of the stories for young people in a colloquial language that can be read to oneself and out loud. These are fables, really, each ending with a moral spoken directly to children.

So, the *Birds and Bats* book was a pleasure to put together—maybe you can imagine what these stories looked like when I discovered them and what I had to do to bring them into the light. It is such pleasure to see them slowly rise out of the dialectal morass in which they were frozen, like so many unsuspecting creatures caught in amber.

Always there are new beginnings. I have completed a third collection and am working on a novel. I'm a little scared; I haven't done a novel since *Plain City*. Novels are my hardest work. They demand so much in terms of the creative process. Unlike collections or biography, every part, of course, must be made by the author. The writer must find the way with words to express a new world. I love and fear that about novel writing. So I don't think about it, not until I'm at the page.

This one I started some time ago and had to put it aside to do something else. There is an opening scene in which something happens which I wasn't certain would fly. It is a kind of intricate trick, and when "CBS Sunday Morning" was down home to do a short piece on me, we set up the trick with some extreme inline skaters. So they filmed it. It was my little research project. And, the trick worked! But CBS took it out of the final cut. Anyway, now I know I can use the trick in the novel.

I have said often enough that, in my vision, the world is full of colors and all colors eventually shade into dark green. Country landscape or, metaphorically, the rural hopescape. The extended family. Stories out of my rural past are told not by one person but by family members, who would enter into a tale and pick it up as it went around the room. Each person, usually a woman, told it in her own way as she remembered it. There was a corrective process of changing, of shaping story, that continued with the round and round telling.

I was definitely influenced by a slew of female talkers who were tale tellers. I was raised by good talkers, my mother the best one among them. These were mothers, elder women friends, grandmothers, and great aunts. And they were a sewing circle called the Jolly Stitchers, who claimed to have made my infant cradle clothes. I never saw them sew a stitch; but often they had one another *in* stitches over a delicious taste of family gossip or household tale.

We girl children rather circled these women folk. They made me feel safe, as they did my cousins, having them always around, always the same good folks. They had a way with words about traditionally female concerns—safety for the children, dealing with illness, birthing, food supplies, caring for home and hearth.

In my memory, women talkers worked with their hands and stayed to home. They were all farm women with strong ways and kind voices. They spoke with delicacy, often calling their own husbands Mister Perry or Mister Turner, for example, in the presence of company. They had odd sensibilities, tastes which we children were quick to gather. And they had keen perceptions and sensitivity to others' expressions of need.

My mother often talked back to herself out loud. She might correct a story, or simply, angry at something, practice what she would say about it.

Words are always on my mind, too. I interrupt their flow and get involved with them by talking back out loud. And then I write words down. Words are always new, always compelling, as they arrange themselves in ways for expressing stories. They allow the stories to suggest emotional truths and to express symbolic possibilities of what life might become for the protagonists. Between past and present of story stands memory. And memory must be one of the pillars of our collective morality. I remind myself to remember what has taken place before I was in place. Reminding myself that there are lives going on that I can talk to and know about. Talk for. I need to remember who took care of me, who raised me, listened to me, soothed me, sang to me, and rocked me. Taught me.

I was reminded of my mother talking back to herself. I missed her, hearing her. Her absence was the inspiration for the *Her Stories* collection. Every book is like a milestone in memory for me. The *Birds* book was a happy accident. There is so much treasure in our collective folkloric heritage, and I literally tripped over Martha Young's contribution.

However, all beginnings lead to those endings which, I hesitate to say, I do not like. We see the truth of endings a hundred times every day. In between the beginning and the ending is the shape of a thing and how we see it. I love the slight of hand, the magic between seeing and enlightenment. I love the play on words having to do with starting and finishing, beginning and ending. We know one another through our words. We start talking, and we finish. I am interested in the fact that we grow more whole by communicating with one another. I'm here because of that. I don't really like public speaking, but I like communicating.

Women, especially gathered together in community, have much to learn from one another. What we have to say makes for very good beginnings and endings, a good story. It delivers us in a common bond of understanding of the story shape in ourselves. Memory is so important to the story of us. We can remember this occasion and, occasionally, Ms. Stein, who was fond of endings. To paraphrase: "She said enough. She said enough. Enough said. She said enough."

Speech given at the Children's Literature New England Conference in Cambridge, Massachusetts, August 1996.

NIKKI GIOVANNI

Urgent Writing

I HAVE, I must confess, had urges to make love. I have definitely had the urge to eat a supreme pizza with everything including extra garlic and anchovies. I have even had the urge to "get away," and have taken off in my car for long, purposeless drives and even once had the urge to go to Alaska to see a glacier. I have never had an urge to write. It is my profession . . . and were I more religiously inclined I might add my calling.

Fortunately I was not called to fry Kentucky chickens nor make little rivets that are ever so important to bridges, nor was there some light in my life that said "Nikki, you will lubricate the chassis," so I have been spared forced enthusiasm for my creations.

Poetry is how I justify the air I take from this planet, the water I waste, people's time when they read my work or hear me do it. Poetry is more than central to me; it is my justification for sharing my belief that each individual is significant and important. It is my midday sun on a winter's day. How has it changed? Children play in winter's sun; retirees sit in the window enjoying the reflected heat; those my age note that we are the middle generation . . . we go forth remembering our past . . . trying to earn our future. We are out of the mold.

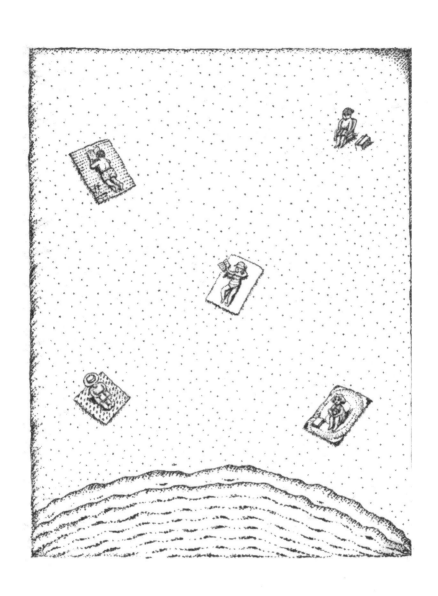

SUMMER READING

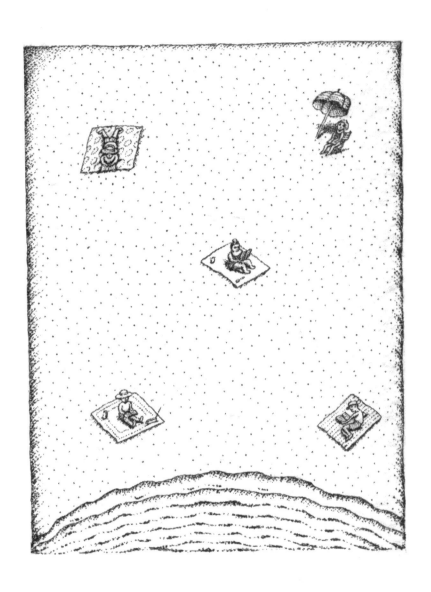

BY PETER SÍS

JACQUELYN MITCHARD

There's a Dance in the Old Dame Yet*

ONCE UPON a time, among storytellers great and small, there was a recipe for literary life. Throughout the kingdom, even in Marin County, all who wrote either espoused it or did not dare to speak in contradiction of it. This is the way I heard it told:

HOW TO BECOME A FAMOUS, YET RESPECTED, NOVELIST

A) Start young. Start real, real young. Write imagaic, nuanced, mercurial, and ingenuous stories for little magazines when you're seventeen. Type them perfectly, on a manual typewriter. At nineteen, go for *Harper's*. Or even *Mademoiselle*.

B) Wow professors until they weep over your talent or make a pass at you, or both. Gender mix does not matter. Quit college to live on angel-hair pasta and breath mints for two years, until you

---

*Donald Marquis.

explode at twenty-three with a searching, bittersweet coming-of-age memoir, featuring funny, but noncriminal, drug use.

C) Get swept away. Prowl Soho, looking for martinis with mushrooms and fetal lemons. Have your picture taken with Jann Wenner. Read only Russians. Study Russian, so you don't need translations. Withdraw for days at a time. If you think you can get away with it, tell *Vanity Fair* it all happened too fast.

D) At thirty-one, bring out the first hundred pages of the great American novel. The other three hundred will be forgiven.

E) When your breakthrough novel is published, be . . . no older than thirty-seven. Buy back your family's ancestral homeplace in Tennessee, even if they actually owned a drugstore in Philly. Gestate a gentle child while the movie is filmed.

Yea, verily, I had heard this tale.

And when, at age forty, I began to write my first novel, *The Deep End of the Ocean*, I believed it with all my heart and with all my soul and with all my mind.

I heard it first in Mark Costello's freshman creative writing class, where beat-like folk from Abilene passed through and read stories to us in which the dark blue of the night sky fell like rain into their mouths. Alan Ginsberg's lover had once lived on their screen porches. Not a stupid girl, I could see that loving the word would not help my demographics. For one thing, as a blue-collar person who dropped her *g*'s, I did not have well-off and bourgeois parents to disdain. I *aspired* to the middle class. I smoked American cigarettes and did not dress all in black. Others in my class were different. Daniel was writing a story about a man searching for a poet after the Apocalypse. Sarah was writing about a girl having a second child by her brother. There was something big going on and really creative, and there were other people born knowing it.

Clearly, on my forehead was writ large that which said, "HACK."

Fast-forward twenty years. I no longer smoke. But the demography has not improved. I'm forty now, widowed, and not glamorously, either. My husband had died young and horribly from cancer the previous year. Dependent on me for support were three sons, four to nine, and a teenage daughter, all catapulted by grief into misery and misbehavior. My hair looked as though it belonged on a teenager selling sunglasses at a mall in Dallas. I weighed about a hundred and too much, and lived in Madison, Wisconsin, in a house that would make John Updike wake up screaming. I not only had a TV, I regularly watched "Thirtysomething" reruns on it, while eating handfuls of cashews. I loved authors such as Wallace Stegner and Willa Cather and even early Stephen King; I could not even parse Thomas Pynchon. And I was a journalist—which, as you know, means having only a single, hard-boiled book in you—which, for the common good, usually remains unwritten.

The only fiction I'd written since college was on job applications.

But the overweening disability, according to me and to myth, was age.

Say I wrote a novel. Say it was even good. I wouldn't live long enough to raise a dynasty—there wasn't enough tread left on me. Nor was I sixteen or seventy, so I did not benefit from the old adage about the dog that walked on its hind legs: The miracle being that it could do the thing at all, much less do it well. There was only one, single luminous Norman MacLean, a legendary late-bloomer.

Enter a dear friend of mine, who happens to be one of the most praised fiction-alists of our generation. It was she who unconvinced me. Though she had herself become a notable during her tender years, she scorned "the recipe" as no more than a way for insecure people to excuse not trying, and to keep the bold from trying, too.

She told me that the story I'd literally dreamed up more than a year before had every right at least to flirt with becoming a book. She told me that despite all those children, all those debts, all that mourning, all that ridiculous hair, I should admit the possibility that a fiction-writing life—as opposed to a ballerina's life—could begin after forty.

This is the part where I should briefly, shamefacedly, admit that my friend also set me up with her agent, her publisher, and many famous book reviewers, who all conspired to make my book an instant success.

But that *would* be fiction.

She gave me the only thing she could give me—gentleness and support. Not the fabled "in."

Consumed with doubt, but having, as Holden Caulfield once put it, a lot of fun in a crummy kind of way, I wrote seventy or so pages of my book.

It was sold by my literary agent, who hadn't represented me on a project in eleven years, and never before on a novel, to the first publisher who saw it; and it did in fact sell lots of copies and got only one rotten and one semi-rotten review, all the rest generous, and the people who had secretly mocked my decision felt amazed (happily, if they were good, and grudgingly, if they were nasty) and screenplay agents who had turned scripts of mine down because (in the words of one), "You're getting started with this kind of . . . late, is all, and plus, you live in like . . . Michigan or somewhere . . ." were sorry they'd passed me by. Book columnists asked me, rather suspiciously, "Where have you been all your life, anyhow?"

What I began hearing was that my book didn't "read" like a first novel. There was a reason for that, and it wasn't sterling prose. It was simply that I had more life on my bones than most firsts. I heard also that I wrote quickly. Again, that was a gift of age. Unlike the young and unencumbered, I hadn't the emotional or economic room for writer's block or simple stalling. And as I learned more, I understood more. More about other great, late bloomers. Like Judith Guest, Erma Bombeck, Mary Wesley, Leo Tolstoy, and Mary Higgins Clark. I learned that the cult of literary wunderkind was too often followed by a lackluster maturity. When an interviewer told me recently, "I was only twenty-two when my first book was published. You're forty-three, so you're too old for success to ruin you," my first impulse was to ask him if his underwear were chafing. My second was to recognize that he was correct. I've been around. I know life has topography, ups followed surely by downs. And I'm ready.

Perhaps I have more than my friend's compassion and my own contrariness to thank. For all the embarrassing things about my babyish Baby Boomer generation, there is the truth that, having taken a tediously long time growing up, we're not going to set any speed records for growing old. This is not all bad. I'm not just talking those stories in the doctor's office magazines about fifty-five-year-old women giving birth to twins. I'm talking successful stockbrokers who go back to school to get certificates to teach third graders to read. Or movie stars who give up their careers to study opera.

Sometimes, it takes years for life to tap you on the shoulder and say, "Surprise! *This* is what you were born for."

What matters about all this is not that I waited until I was overripe to roll the dice, and then that they came up elevens.

What matters is that when literary observers describe the changing colors of the changing scene, they often don't include grays—as in gray hair. Which needs doing, because it is true, as John Prine wrote, that old rivers run wilder every day.

Just as there is room on the field of dreams for people whose surnames are all consonants or whose grandparents risked death by learning to read, there is also room for those of us who might once have been counted out by the stubborn refusal to be daffodils and bloom in the spring. Some have to be roses, who take their time.

CLIFTON L. TAULBERT

Southern Quilts:
Treasured "Kivver" for All

DURING WINTER, when I was a boy, the hot Mississippi Delta sun would retreat to be refueled and the air over the landscape would turn a smoky gray. During this respite from the long, hard summer in the fields, the quilters of the Delta would take the best of old clothes no longer used and create something entirely different and new. Painstakingly patterned and stitched by callused hands, warm, original, patterned quilts emerged and were sent into the future to provide "kivver" for children yet unborn. For the quilt-makers, whose personal worlds were often uncertain and always hard, this task continued season after season.

Although the dominant picture of the South has been painted by the brushes of slavery, Jim Crow, mistrust, and fear, those of us who lived behind that painting also encountered a far richer world, one inhabited by the likes of my great-grand-parents Mama Pearl and Poppa Joe, my Cousin Beauty, our neighbor Miss Doll, and my Aunt Mary Ann, who—in the face of fierce social inequities—showed a remarkable spirit of human resiliency. It was this same resiliency that gave vision to the quilt-makers and was stitched into the fabric of our lives. Every year, they carefully sorted the best of the discarded clothes that had suffered with their wearers through hard times, covering them through bitter nights and backbreaking days, and patched together the quilts we treasured and admired. Those quilts, like the community our elders built around us, placed us far from the reach of those who would try to lay hold of our souls.

I remember as a child helping to pack the finished quilts in a nest of newspapers, boxing them, and tying the cords tightly before we made our annual trek to the "uptown" post office to send them to our relatives up North. It was a ritual older than I and older than my mother—and the delight we took in sending the quilts north was matched by our cousins' joy in receiving them.

Their joy could not have been greater than my own, however, when I received my first quilt after having left the Mississippi Delta at age seventeen to live in the big city of St. Louis. I had long dreamed of the train ride that would take me there and of all that would await me at the end of the journey. However, the reality of the 1960s in urban America showed me a picture far different from the one I had created in my mind. Sleeping in a small room over an equally small St. Louis confectionery, I confronted adulthood in a world far different from the deep South of my youth. Challenged by the city, I missed the people I had left behind. I was grown and couldn't go back, but I wanted so badly to hear those familiar voices once again.

One day a tightly wrapped cardboard box arrived from my great aunt, Ma Ponk. I will always remember how I felt when the neatly stitched "Star of David" quilt came tumbling out of all the newspapers tucked around it. I knew then how my cousins Melvin, Mamie, Mildred, and Earl must have felt when they received the quilts we had sent them from down South. For a few moments, the best of the South surrounded me as I touched each block of material—remembering where I had seen it worn and who had worn it—and then wrapped the quilt around me. I was enveloped by the smell and feel of home, and for a few moments the sounds of the city were lost amid the voices of the quilt.

Just as my personal quilt represented the voices of my elders, their voices would eventually become the fabric of my writings. With my "Star of David" in tow, I left the small St. Louis confectionery and joined the U.S. Air Force, during the time of the Vietnam war. It was at Dow Air Force Base in Maine—as a scared young airman, barely nineteen—that I began to piece a quilt of words, drawn from my childhood in the South, words that would hold me steady and keep my spirit warm. The worse the war became and the more I feared being sent to Vietnam, the more I wrote, losing myself in the voices of the Delta people. From behind the wall of legal segregation, where my people had been both embraced and rebuffed, welcomed and turned away, invited and overlooked, I took the strength, the love, and the resiliency I had known and pieced together quilts that I wished to make into a covering for all—not just for me.

My words and their voices, my memory and their acts became my books—my version of the quilts. My first book, *Once Upon a Time When We Were Colored,* has become a "kivver" for the world, a story of family and human strength. It has been embraced by the likes of South African president Nelson Mandela and Mayor Yossi Peretz of Tiberias, Israel, as well as the people of the South who saw my story grow. Now a well-received motion picture, it was among the films selected for viewing in the 1996 Olympic Village. My people's words and acts became my "kivver," and I feel humbled to have been able to share their warmth and courage with the world.

The life and longing of the South seem to have a permanent place in the halls of literary debate. Known as a place where emotions run deep and feelings are openly worn, it is also a place where the best of the past can be pieced together for the children of the future. The South that has provided me with the words for my quilt is a place where history looms as large as the future and the troubled waters of race relations still need bridges to cross. But I also found universal ideals embedded in the South, a place where your fifteenth cousin is just as much your family as your uncle's firstborn, and where—amid white-pillared mansions that reach for the sky and shotgun houses that keep us anchored to the soil—strong communities, like mine, took root. The South, my homeland, as much as any other place on the planet, still has the opportunity to show the world that something new and different can be created from the joy and pain and contradictions of our lives. The South was the place where my first community was built and the place where I first saw quilts stitched out of suffering, courage, beauty, and hope—treasured "kivver" for us all.

TERRY KAY

TO WHOM THE ANGEL SPOKE: A Story of the Christmas

I have written this story not only to honor the historic celebration of the Christ child as depicted in the scriptures of the New Testament, but also as a declaration that all people—regardless of how different they may seem—are instruments of the miracle of the human experience. It is my hope that the reader will find himself, or herself, in the company of the shepherds, regardless of his, or her, religious persuasion.

ONCE UPON a time, there were three shepherds who lived together to keep watch over their sheep.

Oh, there may have been more than three of them, but that doesn't matter. Three is a good number. Not too few. Not too many.

What does matter is that the three shepherds were good at their work, and their work was not easy. They had to protect their flocks from wild animals, and they had to know where to find fields of deep, thick grass and pools of clean, clear water. They had to know when their sheep were restless and wanted to move about, or when they wanted to rest.

Certainly, the three shepherds knew about sheep.

Still, as people, living together, they were different.

One shepherd was tall.

Another shepherd was short.

The third shepherd was neither tall nor short. He looked short when he stood beside the tall shepherd and tall when he stood beside the short shepherd.

He was in-between. Medium.

One shepherd was fat.

Another shepherd was thin.

The third shepherd was neither fat nor thin. He looked fat when he stood beside the thin shepherd and thin when he stood beside the fat shepherd.

He was in-between. Medium.

One shepherd was black.

Another shepherd was white.

The third shepherd was neither black nor white. His skin was the color of rich bronze, and when he stood beside the black shepherd, he looked curiously pale, but when he stood beside the white shepherd, he looked curiously dark. It was very curious how he looked when he stood between both his friends at the same time— a kind of pale-dark, dark-pale.

You see, he was, well, in-between. Medium.

The three shepherds were different, as all people, everywhere, are different.

Because they were shepherds, they would spend much of their time sitting and relaxing, watching as their sheep huddled in twos and threes and fours to graze from the grass.

As they sat and relaxed, the shepherds would sometimes sing songs they knew—different songs, often at the same time—and the sheep would look at them with puzzled faces as if to say, "What strange men are these shepherds who watch over us."

Sometimes, when they were not singing, they would grumble and argue among themselves.

"It is!" one shepherd would say.

"It is not!" another shepherd would reply.

"I don't know. If it is, it is. If it is not, it is not," the third shepherd would suggest.

"Well, I say it is."

"And I say it is not."

"And I don't know."

The three shepherds loved to argue—about anything.

And if they were not singing or arguing or polishing the crooks of their long shepherd's sticks, they would lie quietly in the spongy quilts of grass and listen to the sheep and imagine the sheep were speaking to them in an unknown language, telling them secrets no one had ever heard. Or they would listen to the wind whistle as it dipped and soared through the hills.

One shepherd said the wind made him lonely. He thought a man should have a home and not wander like a nomad through the hills.

"I don't like it, being out here," he complained. "Sleeping on the grass, like sheep. A person should have a place to go to at nighttime. He should have a table to sit at when eating his food. He should have a bed—a warm bed on cold nights."

Another shepherd said the wind made him restless. He thought he should have been a world traveller. Perhaps a trader. Someone who carried cloth to the seas and returned with spices from the city.

"Ah, that would have been a wonderful life," he said, dreamily. "To see the great cities of the world, to travel the great roads, to meet the great people in great places. That's better than staying in the hills, looking at sheep day after day."

The third shepherd—the in-between, medium one—said he didn't really think about the wind. It was part of being a shepherd, and, after all, that's what he was: a shepherd.

"Sometimes I would like to have a home and a table and a bed," he said to his friends. "Sometimes I would like to travel to the great cities on the great roads and meet the great people, but most of the time, it doesn't matter. I'm a shepherd. I don't mind being here in the hills."

They were very different, these three men who were shepherds.

One shepherd had been complaining about the new tax that the king, whose name was Herod, had demanded from the people.

"He's nothing but a money-grabber," he shouted loudly from the hills—knowing no one except the other two shepherds could hear him. "Why can't he pick on the rich? Bah! I'll not pay! He's a madman who should be made to live with swine. I'll not pay, I tell you. Taxes are high enough. Let them try to find me here in the hills! Let them send their soldiers. I won't pay!"

Another shepherd disagreed.

"We should pay," he argued. "Look how King Herod keeps away our enemies. True, he may be a pompous old man, but still he gives us something in return. All of that costs money. Soldiers can't feed on grass, like sheep. They can't fight far-away wars with sticks and stones. They need weapons. I don't mind paying. And if I had a home, I'd pay even more than they ask."

"Bah!" his companion roared. "He oppresses our people. We bow before him like dogs whining before their masters for bread crumbs. If I could travel over the world, to the great cities, I am sure I would find kings who do not oppress their people."

The third shepherd said he didn't care one way or the other. He didn't want to pay the tax, but he would if he had to.

His attitude was—well, in-between.

"I know so little about kings and soldiers and faraway wars," he confessed.

The only thing the third shepherd was curious about was the constant caravan of people going into the small town of Bethlehem to pay the tax of Herod.

"I did not know so many had moved away," he said quietly. "I wonder if any of them are old friends. Perhaps I played with some of them as a boy. I wonder if I would remember any of them. It's been such a long time since I was a boy."

He smiled softly and added, "I remember playing hide-and-seek. I could hide in such places that no one could find me."

One of the other shepherds laughed.

"So that's where your sheep learned their hiding tricks," he said.

And, so, the three men who were shepherds sat on the top of a hill overlooking Bethlehem and watched the faraway, thin line of people moving slowly along a rough, dusty road toward the town.

"Fools!" yelled the angry shepherd, jabbing his shepherd's crook into the ground. "You're wasting your money on a tyrant."

"Faithful!" his friend called out, laughing and making fun of the first shepherd. "Be glad you have kings and soldiers to watch over you."

"I wish I were closer, so I might see who they are," sighed the third shepherd— the in-between one—as he gazed at the little haze of dust puffed up by the slow feet of men and animals.

Oh, yes, they were very, very different, the three men who were shepherds.

Everyone who lived back then—back in the time of the three shepherds— remembered the night.

Sunset opened in a splatter of color—orange and red and purple. Slender streams of light reaching out from the palm of the sun, reaching out high and long to catch something in their bright fingers. Trees. Hills. The buildings of Bethlehem. Something. Anything.

The three shepherds marveled at the sunset. They stood, side by side—the in-between shepherd standing in-between the tall shephard and the short shepherd— and they cupped their hands over their eyes to shade out the glare. The light settled over them and threw their shadows—tall, in-between, short shadows—against the mountain.

"Beautiful!" said one shepherd.

"Magnificent!" said another shepherd.

"Wonderful!" said the third shepherd.

For one rare moment, the three had agreed on something.

Even the sheep, which usually had little concern for such things, looked at the sunset. Some of them bleated. All of them looked.

And then the sunset disappeared and stars began to pop out against the blot of darkness. The stars sparkled and flamed and seemed to dance with brightness.

"I see bad weather in this night," said one of the shepherds, as he prepared to raise a tent.

"I think it is a good omen," said another shepherd. "I think we will have days of good grazing, valleys of thick grass, and flowing streams of water."

"I do not know," said the third shepherd. "If it is not one, perhaps it will be the other."

The brightness kept the shepherds awake.

One was afraid.

Another was fascinated.

The third was curious.

And the sheep were restless.

"I think this is strange," said the black shepherd—or it might have been the white shepherd, or even the bronze shepherd; anyway, one of them said it. "I think above us is the brightest star the heavens ever held."

His friends nodded.

"Yes," said one.

"Quite so," said the other.

Again, the three shepherds had agreed on something.

The star above them glittered like a brilliant, giant jewel turning with the wind. It caught the light of the moon and the other stars and threw the light toward earth, toward Bethlehem.

The three shepherds whispered in awe, each saying the same thing:

"Look . . ."

". . . Look."

". . . Look."

And as they were watching the star pour down its golden light upon Bethlehem and the hills around Bethlehem, the three shepherds heard something that sounded like a voice—words from the throat of the wind, rushing up from a distant valley, sliding over the lap of the hills in a whistling cry like the gathering of a sudden storm.

"What was that?" cried one of the shepherds.

"A voice. I know it. A—a windvoice," muttered the second shepherd.

"Yes, I heard it, too," whispered the third shepherd. "It—it said something like—like, '*Fear not.*'"

"Yes, yes, that was it," the first shepherd agreed. "'*Fear not.*' But why am I so afraid?"

The three shepherds moved closer together, huddling like their sheep, and listened.

They heard the rushing sound of the windvoice again—mightier than before—and the light of the star rolled over them, and the three shepherds fell to the ground, terribly frightened. They threw their cloaks over their faces, trying to hide from the light and the windvoice.

The fat shepherd began mumbling prayers learned long ago, as a child.

The thin shepherd began singing a psalm of David taught to him by his mother.

The third shepherd—who was neither fat nor thin—began chanting praises he had heard from travellers.

And then the windvoice became loud and clear. It said again:

"*Fear not: for, behold, I bring you good tidings of great joy, which shall be to all people.*"

The three shepherds hugged each other in fear.

"Oh, what is happening?" they cried, trembling so hard they were bumping heads.

And again the voice surrounded them:

"*For unto you is born this day in the City of David a Saviour, which is Christ the Lord. And this shall be a sign unto you: Ye shall find the Babe wrapped in swaddling clothes, lying in a manger.*"

Then, out of the heavens, the shepherds heard other voices—voices that exploded and echoed throughout the hills:

"*Glory to God in the highest, and on earth peace, good will toward men.*"

And then the voices were gone, leaving a silence as still as morning, untouched and clean. The three shepherds pulled off their cloaks from over their faces and looked at one another.

"How could this be?" whispered one.

"I do not know," said another. "How can voices come out of the wind? Does the wind know how to speak?"

"But it did," said the third. "It was the voice of the Lord. It had to be. Did we not hear the words?"

The other shepherds agreed:

"Yes."

"Yes."

The three shepherds sat and listened to the silence and stared at the star burning in the sky above them.

"It brings all of the light of the other stars to it," said one shepherd.

"I think it is the sun, which has broken apart," guessed another shepherd.

"Why did its light fall on us?" asked the third shepherd.

Then one of them said, "Let us go now even unto Bethlehem, and see this thing, which is come to pass, which the Lord hath made known unto us."

"Yes, I agree," said another of the shepherds.

"Yes, let us go," said the third shepherd.

And, so, the three shepherds went into Bethlehem, following the bright path of the brightest star above them, and they came to a place where the child who would be named Jesus lay, wrapped in swaddling clothes as the windvoice had promised.

One by one, they bowed quietly before the child, and then each went away to tell a different story of what had happened, because the three shepherds—those to whom the angel spoke—were different, as all people, everywhere, are different.

Yet, they heard a voice one night, and because they believed what the voice told them, they were alike.

And again that voice speaks. To all who are different, but are seekers and askers and believers, that voice is heard always at the Christmas. It says, as it said to the three shepherds:

"For unto you is born this day in the City of David a Saviour, which is Christ the Lord."

Amen. Amen.

JANE YOLEN

GRANDDAUGHTER

Wet like an otter sliding down a known path
into the posturing reeds,
eely bones not yet hard,
you slipped into my life.
I did not know what to call you:
animal, vegetable, mineral,
that old game of guesses
we played on ninety-seventh street.

Ten perfect fingers, ten perfect toes,
the doctor's rote was like hot pepper jumprope,
like silver-colored stars
scattered across the pavement,
onesies, twosies, a jack caught in a grating,
allie-allie-home-free,
the suddenness of my own forgotten childhood
caught up in your tiny, grasping hand.

MARK GERZON

Beyond the Divided States

from *A House Divided: Six Belief Systems Struggling for America's Soul*

I pledge allegiance to the flag of my State,
and to the belief system for which it stands,
one State, invincible,
with liberty and justice for us.

THIS IS obviously not the Pledge of Allegiance we recited as children. It does not reflect the original patriotism of the founders of this country. On the contrary, it reflects the narrow and short-sighted patriotism of the Divided States that has taken root in America. Many of us have either forgotten the words to the original pledge, or forgotten what it means—if, in fact, we ever knew.

The founders of this nation knew that loyalty to a state, rather than to the Union of all states, would set us on a dangerous course. Indeed, when states seceded from the Union during the Civil War, the following bloodbath left wounds in our national psyche yet unhealed. Just as we don't give our ultimate loyalty to Pennsylvania or Georgia, so we cannot give our ultimate loyalty to Patria or Gaia. California may be where we live, and Corporatia may reflect what we believe, but to neither of them can we, as Americans, pledge our final allegiance.

The actual Pledge of Allegiance says this:

> *I pledge allegiance to the flag of the* United *States of America,*
> *and to the republic for which it stands,*
> one *nation,* indivisible,
> *under God,*
> *with liberty and justice for* all.[1]

If we compare the actual Pledge of Allegiance to the distorted one, we witness the challenge America faces. The six belief systems described in [*A House Divided*] are pitting citizen against citizen, dividing us. It isn't a question of whether one of the Divided States is right, and the others is wrong. They are *all* right—and *all* wrong. In almost all public policy controversies, the antagonists represent different aspects of the real truth. To split serious, committed citizens into opposing groups—using knee-jerk, meat-cleaver rhetoric of right versus wrong or Right vs. Left—is a travesty of democratic dialogue. For new patriots, the challenge is to defend the complexity of the truth. Unlike *part*isans, who stand up for only *part* of the truth, new patriots strive to represent the whole.

The question is: how do these competing belief systems, and the scores of variations and combinations of them, coexist in a democracy?

Patriotism Must Be a Living Force, Growing and Changing Like the Country Itself.

The answer, in a word, is patriotism. But the new patriotism which America so urgently needs is not the old-fashioned, I'm-right, you're-wrong, love-it-or-leave-it kind of patriotism that caused so much turmoil during this century. Catalyzing the gifts of all of the States, and restraining the dangers they pose, will be the challenge of the twenty-first-century patriotism. But before we can meet that challenge, we must understand the old patriotism—and break free.

Twentieth-Century Patriotism
"LOVE IT OR LEAVE IT"

The second half of the twentieth century has witnessed a growing awareness of the paradoxes buried deep within the old patriotism. The paradoxes turned vicious in the fifties with McCarthyism, and exploded in the headlines again during the sixties in the struggles over civil rights and the Vietnam war. During the years of war in Vietnam, the old patriotism was wielded like a club to force people into conformity. To tell a young person that he or she should be "more patriotic" often meant supporting, rather than questioning, the war effort. Because challenging the legitimacy of the war was considered by many to be unpatriotic, they drew a line in the sand: from their perspective, hawks were patriotic, doves weren't.

Patriotism, alas, was frequently reduced to partisanship. It became synonymous, not with love of one's country, but with support for a specific war. Those who did not agree with the controversial government policy toward Vietnam were subjected to epithets that implied they were somehow un-American. Slogans such as "My country, right or wrong" and "America: Love it or leave it" were used to imply that those who opposed the war were no longer entitled to American citizenship. Meanwhile, dissenters sometimes called their fellow citizens who supported the war "pigs," "fascists," and worse. They spit on the flag and equated patriotism with mindless, Nazi-like obedience.

Vietnam was not the only influence that undermined the old patriotism. Government deceit, fraud, and corruption, combined with the Watergate lawlessness, also fueled cynicism and distrust. In addition, the civil rights movement under the leadership of Reverend Martin Luther King, Jr., catalyzed Americans' awareness of the gap between democratic ideals and racist realities. All these combined during the Vietnam era to undermine the old patriotism.

The old concept of patriotism fell into disrepute and was used less frequently. But it didn't disappear: it splintered. Its underlying belief is inherent in each of the Divided States. In essence, its message: If you don't share my belief system, then you aren't a patriot.

The Old Patriotism Preached Freedom
But Practiced Conformity.

The old patriots expected uniformity, that is, one relatively narrow set of identities. Senators could not be African-American; Miss Americas could not be deaf; sports heroes could not be gay. Limited diversity was accepted only if it could be adapted to the traditional way of life. Despite our rhetoric about freedom and equality, those who didn't fit fell outside the definition of patriotic Americans.

The old patriotism's demand for uniformity all too frequently led to a kind of hypocrisy, even in the Declaration of Independence. "As a nation we began by declaring that 'all men are created equal,'" wrote Abraham Lincoln to his friend

Joshua F. Speed almost a century after the Declaration was written. "We now practically read it 'All men are created equal except Negroes.'" In terms of the right to vote, for example, it took another century—and the deaths of hundreds of thousands of Americans in the Civil War—before dark-skinned men were given the same rights as white-skinned men. It took another half-century before women of any color were allowed to enter the voting booth. So deep was this hypocrisy that, at the ceremony unveiling the Lincoln Memorial in Washington, D.C., more than a half-century after Lincoln's death, African-Americans in the audience were segregated from whites. In other words, there was—and still is— a significant gap between what the Declaration of Independence preached and what we, the people, have practiced.

Built into the old patriotism, then, was a split between those Americans who were included and those who were not. Over generations the boundary shifted, but it never disappeared. As a result, exclusion has always been part of our history. Those who did not fit were by definition "un-American" (commies, troublemakers, rabble-rousers, secret agents, agitators, nigger-lovers, traitors) and had to be shunned, exiled, imprisoned, or killed. Patriotic Americans would avoid association with these unpatriotic, dangerous elements in our society.

Consequently, the basic attitudes of this conformity-based old patriotism were intolerance and disrespect toward those different from us. Both the McCarthyism of the fifties and the die-hard racial segregationism of the sixties are recent examples of the old patriotism in action. Incredible pressure was put on Americans to conform to a set of attitudes. Intolerance was turned into a virtue. At its worst, the old patriotism considered it heroic to destroy the reputations of those whose political attitudes were deemed "un-American."

To confirm that the old patriotism is still with us, simply open your newspaper or watch the evening news on television. Public discourse today reflects the corrosive impact of the old patriotism. The prevalent debating style is characterized by increasing hostility. Shouting is common; blame is everywhere. Wherever one turns—from the talk show on the car radio to prime-time TV, from the political speech to the televangelist's sermon, from the high-profile court case to the city council meeting—the level of public discourse seems to be deteriorating. The more vicious the talk show host, the larger his audience. The more angrily someone trashes another, the longer the sound bite. The uglier the campaign, the more air time the candidates receive. None of the Divided States are raising the level of discourse in America, yet all complain loudly that it is falling into the gutter.

The Blind Obedience of the Old Patriotism
Has Corroded into Cynicism.

While once the old patriotism led to faith in America, today it has eroded into cynicism. Citizens of the Divided States, who care more about their belief systems than about their country, become painfully cynical about their fellow citizens. And cynicism, in its most extreme form, is the opposite of patriotism.

"Cynical" means: "Marked by or displaying contemptuous mockery of the motives or virtues of others: a cynical attitude toward society."[2] Being cynical implies that we expect to be treated badly by each other, and cynicism leads us to confirm those expectations. We expect anyone who is not a citizen of our Divided State to "rip us off." We expect politicians to be liars, the advertiser to mislead us, the salesman to be disreputable, the policeman to be corrupt or brutal, the lawyer to be unscrupulous, the government worker to be lazy, the teacher to be ineffective, the doctor to overcharge, the news reporter to sensationalize, the New Age guru to be a fraud, and the televangelist to embezzle.

This is far from what cynicism originally meant. Founded by a student of Socrates in the fifth century B.C., the school of philosophy called cynicism established an austere, independent way of thinking that would not be corrupted by social conventions or material pursuits. Even today, cynicism can be a life-saving antidote to naiveté, gullibility, and ignorance. Instead of blindly believing in unworthy leaders, unjust policies, or hand-me-down ideologies, postwar generations adopted the attitude summarized by the bumper sticker: QUESTION AUTHORITY. Such cynicism helped expose many ills, embarrass demagogues, expose widely believed untruths, and improve many of our institutions.

But too much cynicism, like too much salt, can spoil what it was supposed to enhance. That is precisely what has happened to citizenship in America in the closing third of this century. When the Gallup poll in 1990 asked voters in what institutions they had "a great deal" or "quite a lot" of confidence, their replies revealed how far cynicism had diminished our faith in each other and in our institutions. Only 13 percent had confidence in political parties, 18 percent in business, 18 percent in the federal government, 20 percent in state government, and 23 percent in local (municipal) government. In 1994, just four years later, when the Daniel Yankelovich Group (DYG, Inc.) asked the same questions, cynicism had corroded citizenship even more deeply. Confidence had dropped even further: confidence in political parties was 11 percent; in national business leaders, 15 percent; in the federal government, 16 percent; and in state government, 19 percent. Even the trust in institutions that have traditionally inspired faith, such as the churches, dropped precipitously during this decade.[3]

In a democracy, such cynicism is extremely dangerous. Self-government depends on the involvement of citizens and on their confidence in public institutions. When that confidence erodes, eaten away by resentment, bitterness, and apathy, democracy becomes an empty shell. Democracy is "vulnerable to the erosion of meaning in its institutions," observed Peter Berger and Richard John Neuhaus. "Cynicism threatens it; wholesale cynicism can destroy it."[4]

As mistrust rises, the bonds of citizenship fray. When these bonds are overly weakened, society breaks down. Almost two out of three Americans in 1994 believed that their communities were unhealthy because of a lack of public accountability and a lack of shared values and vision, and because "everyone is looking out for themselves."[5] Or as the Iowan farmer Jim Rohlfsen said: "We're all looking at what's good for us, not the country. . . . Everybody is their own lobby."

The Old Patriotism, Now an Anachronism, Breeds a Politics of Polarization.

Since the old patriotism requires conformity and excludes those who do not conform, politics has become increasingly polarized. Based on competing ideologies which separate all issues into pro or con, left or right, and patriotic or unpatriotic, it has become increasingly out of touch with the complexity of modern life. This breeds division among citizens, pitting partisans on both extremes against each other. Repelled by the political game, the majority of citizens have become merely spectators. The result is low voter turnout and widespread despair about the political process and America's future.

In Hawkins County, Tennessee, a fundamentalist Christian mother objected to her sixth-grade daughter's reading a science fiction story in school in which astronauts encounter Martians who communicate telepathically. Offended by what she perceived to be a New Age, anti-Christian story line, this offended parent helped catalyze a conflict between conservative Christians, on the one hand, and liberal defenders of free speech on the other. After four years of litigation and more than $1.5 million in lawyers' fees, the involvement of national organizations like Concerned Women of America and People for the American Way, intensified hostility and divisiveness in the community, and an increasingly polarized educational system, nothing was gained. Trust had eroded; money had been wasted.

"The conclusion I draw," says lawyer Stephen Bates, who studied the case in detail, "is that *everyone* lost. . . ."[6]

In hundreds of school districts, parents, teachers, and school administrators are spending precious dollars and even more precious time and energy in battles that do little to strengthen their children's education. Everyone loses—except, of course, the legal profession. "Does America really need 70 percent of the world's lawyers?" former vice president Dan Quayle asked. Most Americans clearly don't think so. In a *National Law Journal* poll, three out of four Americans said there are too many lawyers for our own good. From the Right to the Left, concerned citizens sense that the old patriotism needs to be overhauled. Our combative ways of solving our civic problems must change.[7]

Hypocrisy, hostility, cynicism, division, blame—the result of these ugly features of the old patriotism is gridlock. Moderate lawmakers of both parties have been thrown out of office, and political experts across the political spectrum predict several years of stalemates. Dan Mitchell, a political analyst at the conservative Heritage Institution, foresees "gridlock in the true sense of the word. . . . Neither side will have the power to get anything all the way through."[8] "People are as discouraged about politics as they have ever been," observed a front-page *New York Times* article based on scores of interviews across the country. The condition of the country was captured in the headline: "Anger and Cynicism Well Up in Voters as Hope Gives Way."[9]

A few days before the 1994 elections, the Associated Press asked Americans whether they would rather see the Republicans take control of Congress or see the Democrats keep control. The people split evenly, one out of four wanting Republicans at the helm and the same percentage wanting the Democrats. The surprising news was that 42 percent said that, no matter who won, it wouldn't make much difference.[10]

In poll after poll, most Americans preferred that Republicans and Democrats work together for the good of the country; and said they were tired of petty bickering and polarized political maneuvering, were angry with Congress, and wanted real leadership. But the same polls showed that people were pessimistic and cynical, afraid nothing would change; and that polarizing, self-serving "politics as usual" would continue.

Twenty-First Century Patriotism
"A UNION OF HEARTS AND HANDS"

As we contrast the old and the new patriotism, let us not be confused. Just as the past and the present are both within us, so are the old and the new patriotism. On the edge of the next millennium, they are struggling for our souls.

Before we reject the old patriotism, let us remind ourselves of its virtues. Behind its rigid and sometimes cruel conformity, for example, was cohesion, which held the nation together. The old patriotism, it is true, suffered from hypocrisy, but that was a result of the Founding Fathers' idealism, a vision of equality and justice so perfect that no nation on earth has yet achieved it. And yes, the old patriotism led to gridlock, but it also provided stability: a century since the Civil War with far less internal strife than in many other nations.

The old patriotism has clearly played a vital role in the experiment called America. But now our generation is called to reinvent democracy, as Jefferson predicted each generation would be. We can't just substitute one set of attitudes for another. We can't just follow a new leader, or join a new political party. The change required is deeper.

If the Divided States are struggling for America's soul, then the struggle is also happening within each of us—that is, at the deepest level of our beings, where what we hold sacred resides.

Although today it is easy to forget, patriotism is about love. It means loving one's country—the whole, complex, beautiful and ugly, amazing kaleidoscope of human beings who call themselves Americans. And as we all know from our own lives, there is more than one way to love—and there is more than one way to be a patriot.

A "pledge" is more than just a statement of belief. To pledge means to "promise solemnly," and to "stake one's life, honor, word"; or, as another dictionary phrases it, it means "a formal promise to do something."[1] And what we do, if it is truly patriotic, must be done out of love, not out of hate. As Martin Luther King, Jr., said when he accepted the Nobel Peace Prize: "Man must evolve for all human conflict a method which rejects revenge, aggression, and retaliation. The foundation of such a method is love." And this is the common denominator of the new patriotism: to promise to do something out of love for the whole country.

The New Patriotism Is Rooted In Love, Not Hate.

Just doing something is easy; the citizens of the Divided States "do something" every day. But doing something out of love for the whole country is hard. It involves our souls. It is so hard to do that even the wisest, most enlightened, and most compassionate men and women of our times find it challenging, and sometimes impossible.

One of the people who has described what loving one's whole country requires is Thich Nhat Hanh, a Vietnamese priest who during the Vietnam war was part of a Buddhist fellowship that tried to minister to the needs of both sides. Because they tried to care for the souls of both pro-communist and anti-communist forces alike, many priests were killed. His work, for which Martin Luther King, Jr., nominated him for the Nobel Peace Prize, was based on the following philosophy:

> To reconcile conflicting parties, we must have the ability to understand the suffering of both sides. If we take sides, it is impossible to do the work of reconciliation. And humans want to take sides. That is why the situation gets worse and worse. Are there people who are still available to both sides? They need not do much. They need do only one thing: go to one side and tell all about the suffering endured by the other side, and go to the other side and tell all about the suffering endured by this side. That is our chance for peace. That can change the situation. But how many of us are able to do that?

This philosophy, which would be utterly alien to the old patriotism, is the cornerstone of the new. It is a new standard of citizenship that requires that, if we love our country, we must at least respect its citizens—even if we disagree fundamentally with them. As Lincoln advised us:

> Let us neither express nor cherish any hard feelings toward any citizen who . . . has differed with us. Let us at all times remember that all American citizens are brothers of a common country, and should dwell together in the bonds of fraternal feeling.[12]

Such "fraternal feeling"—which Lincoln elsewhere called "a Union of hearts and hands"—is a kind of love. It is rooted not just in the mind or even the heart, but also in the soul. It requires the deepest and most profound commitment of which we are capable. Fortunately, unlike pioneers such as Reverend King and Thich Nhat Hanh, most of us do not have to risk our lives. But we do have to take risks. We have to stretch ourselves to embrace the sacred dimension of citizenship. The Golden Rule that appears in every major religion is also the Golden Rule of patriotism: treating others the way we ourselves want to be treated.

Like the earlier pioneers who spread America westward, the new patriots who are developing this faith are spiritual pioneers.[13] They are committed to learning, not dogmatism. One of the reasons the Founding Fathers placed such an emphasis on publicly funded education was that they knew a democracy depended on continued learning. Thomas Jefferson underscored its importance when he wrote:

> I know of no safe repository of the ultimate powers of the society but the people themselves; and if we think them not enlightened enough to exercise control with a wholesome discretion, the remedy is not to take it from them, but to inform their discretion by education.[14]

Applied to patriotism, learning is critical. If we listen to many conflicting opinions, as Thich Nhat Hanh advises us to do, learning is inevitable. The premise of the new patriotism is that in virtually all conflicts the opposing parties each hold a piece of the truth. Helping the different sides find common ground requires bringing those pieces together into a coherent whole—and that requires a willingness to learn.

From the outset, diversity is at the heart of the new patriotism. It assumes that there is no single way to be an American. "It is a common belief," says Mayor Frederic Peralta of Taos, New Mexico, "that 'all-American' means baseball, hot dogs, the Fourth of July, and apple pie. We now understand that these beliefs aren't entirely correct. It also means enchiladas, sopapillas, powwows, fiestas, and more."[15]

To incorporate this growing diversity, we must learn as citizens—politically, psychologically, culturally, intellectually, and spiritually. Our generation, and those that follow, must let go of the notion of racial, ethnic, or religious purity; let go of the comfortable image of a "melting pot" (in which "others" melt down into a homogeneous "us"); and let go of other static metaphors (like "mosaic" or "salad bowl"). Instead, we must view America with the humility and wonder with which a child looks through a kaleidoscope. What we behold is constantly changing, with an infinite number of combinations.[16]

This magnificent diversity, though hard to encompass in our fixed ideologies, may turn out in the end to be the key to our survival. Just as the history of the planet shows that biodiversity is the key to evolutionary survival, so may social diversity be a key to human progress, if—repeat *if*—we will let it.

In opposing California's Proposition 187, the so-called "anti-immigrant" ballot initiative, Republican leader Jack Kemp spoke of the Statue of Liberty and its welcome to the world's refugees. He advised his fellow Republicans to make their party "the party of immigrants . . . the party of men and women who seek civil and legal and voting and equal rights." It was good advice, not just for his party, but for his country. It is not just the challenge of Republicans or Democrats to become "inclusionary, not exclusionary," to use Kemp's phrase, but a challenge for every one of us who call ourselves Americans.[17]

Honoring diversity can lead to a wide range of views about policy issues such as immigration, affirmative action, bilingual education, and a host of other thorny issues. But what it requires of all of us is a personal integrity—an acknowledgment of our own imperfections, the willingness to see situations as a whole, and a recognition of our adversaries' positions as well as our own.

Universal though the Golden Rule may be, it is rarely practiced. This is the challenge which the new patriotism must meet. If we believe that "all men [and women] are created equal," then we must practice what we preach. We cannot exclude vast numbers of American citizens, and regard them as enemies. Instead of excluding others, the new patriots are reaching out to work with them. As citizens, we must act in accordance with the ideals on which our country is founded, whatever the views we may hold on particular policies. To do this requires tolerance and respect for others who differ from us, however difficult this may sometimes seem.

The nation in which we live is far, far different from the one the Founding Fathers began more than 200 years ago. When the nation was founded, the overwhelmingly white and European population considered itself homogeneous. Three-fifths were English, one-tenth German, and the remainder a European potpourri. The indigenous peoples and the black slaves were not counted. The nation's early leaders felt confident that American citizens would continue to be white Protestants primarily of British origin.[18]

By the 1800 census, however, the population of just over five million was already one-fifth African-American. One hundred years later, the population of over seventy-five million included Chinese, Japanese, and the now recognized "Indians." In the period between 1819 to 1955 over forty million aliens entered the United States, a migration of truly epic proportions. As diverse as the immigrants were, however, still more than three out of four had originated in Europe.

Today, this is no longer true. By the mid-eighties, the flow of immigrants from England, which once represented the vast majority of newcomers, had dwindled. Mexicans, Filipinos, Koreans, Cubans, Indians, Chinese, Dominicans, Vietnamese, Jamaicans, Haitians, Iranians—all contributed more new citizens than the English. With new immigrants arriving during the 1990s at a projected average of nearly 900,000 a year, demographers foresee that by the year 2000 the proportion of whites among America's children will shrink to less than two-thirds. It is already half or less in three states: Texas, California, and New Mexico. By the middle of the next century, no ethnic or racial group will constitute a majority. The number of Hispanics will surpass the number of blacks within two decades.[19] By the middle of the twenty-first century the once predominant ethnic group—white Europeans—will become a minority.

America's kaleidoscope of ethnic, racial, and ideological diversity has unfortunately been accompanied by hostility, disrespect, prejudice, and violence.

The New Patriotism Embraces, Rather Than Denies, America's Exploding Diversity.

The alternative to hostility is civility. Civility doesn't mean keeping our mouths shut. It does not mean lying about our true feelings, or even "settling for half." Civility implies cultivating personal humility rather than indulging in self-righteousness, and valuing tolerance rather than force. Whether a conflict is between Koreans and blacks in South Central Los Angeles, or between pro-life and pro-choice advocates outside an abortion clinic in Tallahassee, or between irate townspeople and the city council, the new patriots facing such conflicts remain civil. They do not abandon their beliefs; they can still get angry at their adversaries. But they know that Americans are connected to each other by this cord of courtesy. Once the cord is broken, it is hard to repair.

Nan Aron, director of the liberal advocacy group Alliance for Justice, put it bluntly when she said that groups like hers profit from "being able to point to a monster."[20] But the problem is: the monster is *us*, including our neighbors—our fellow Americans. Unlike the old patriots who took sides, joined their respective armies, picked up their weapons, and started firing at the "enemy," the new patriots face a tougher task. For them, ostracizing their fellow Americans is not an acceptable option. Whether they vote for one party or another, whether they are pro-this or anti-that, their country comes first. They know that America's strength depends on finding legitimate common ground among adversaries.

This cannot be accomplished through the conventional hit-and-run, punch-and-counterpunch style of public discourse that is so prevalent in political campaigning and media-sponsored debate. New patriots do not engage in shouting matches with their adversaries, but listen to them with the same attention that they expect from their own listeners. If there's an impasse, they try to analyze what each party has contributed to it and to find a common solution.

These virtues are easy to preach, but extremely difficult to practice. Genuine patriotism has never been easy—not for the revolutionaries of 1776, not for the men and women who defended America against aggression in the 1940s, and not today, as the new patriots attempt to protect America against subtle threats from within. Instead of being cynical, which provides an excuse for doing nothing, the new patriots attempt to involve themselves in the affairs of their communities. [Later in *A House Divided*], we will turn to some of their stories, showing what an impact genuine citizenship can have.

The New Patriotism Inspires Collaboration and Partnership.

To understand how vital the new patriots are to our future, allow yourself to imagine for a moment that you are a patient on an operating table. You overhear that three out of four members of the surgical team agree on how your operation should be performed, but the fourth vehemently disagrees. Do you feel comforted—or afraid? Or imagine that you are a resident in a burning building. You see the firemen discussing outside how to put out the fire and hear that over half of them agree to cooperate. Do you feel relieved—or angry?

Some tasks, and some occasions, require a high degree of partnership. Most of the challenges we face today simply cannot be achieved with 51 percent support. They require of us all a capacity to oppose or to challenge each other while at the same time working with and respecting each other. The new patriots put the country first—the *whole* country—and their citizenship is sacred to them.

Precisely what they believe, however, varies enormously. The new patriots do not have unanimous opinions. The increasingly heterogeneous human beings who call themselves Americans cannot fit the white, Anglo-Saxon, Protestant stereotype of yesteryear. Today, the "national conversation" includes people of many languages, not just English; people of various colors, not just white and black; people of many educational levels, not just the literati; and of many income groups, not just the affluent; not just the "old boys network," but women and gays as well; and, as we have seen, with many competing belief systems.

Consequently, our future must be based on partnership, not polarization. Just as a healthy dose of skepticism about our political adversaries is necessary to the political process, there always will be a place for partisanship in democracy. In a democracy, interests are often pitted against each other. Our system of checks and balances is designed to mediate these conflicts and yield acceptable compromises. To be partisan—that is, to argue strongly on behalf of your interests as against someone else's—is a vital part of citizenship.

Obviously the new patriotism will not resolve all our domestic conflicts. Of course, in a complex world, individuals will inevitably become polarized in their response to issues, as they seek to define their positions. Of course, in a two-party system, partisans will clash as they seek legislative solutions to pressing problems. But the emerging twenty-first-century patriotism will keep us focused on the larger challenge of rebuilding the bonds that connect us to each other and to our country.

Transforming partisan polarization into patriotic partnership is clearly a challenge to every State, every belief system, and every American. The easy way out—to call one's adversaries dirty names and walk away—is dragging America down. The challenge is to join the new patriots who are turning enemies into allies. Anyone who thinks the process of enabling enemies to become partners is quick or easy has never witnessed the process. It is long and difficult and fraught with danger. It is not a magical transformation, but an act of the deepest will, compassion, and civic courage.

When we stop trying to destroy our adversaries and acknowledge that they too are part of American life, they then become merely competitors, as athletes are; and we find ourselves competing against worthy opponents who actually share our goals. Ultimately, our rivals may even become our partners, when they recognize that, despite appearances, we need them and depend on them. To evolve from enemies to adversaries, from adversaries to rivals, and from rivals to partners—this is part of the challenge of the new patriotism.[21]

The New Patriotism in Action
UNITING THE STATES

The contrast between the old and new patriotism should now be clear; at least in theory: learning, instead of conformity; diversity, instead of uniformity; integrity, not hypocrisy; partnership, not partisanship. But words are not enough.

What makes these concepts of a new patriotism meaningful are the ordinary citizens who turn them into action. The new patriots step out of the narrow confines of their comfort zones—their belief systems, their race, their religion, in other words, their Divided States—and explore their interconnection with their fellow Americans. Some do so out of principle; but many others do so out of sheer necessity—simply because it has to be done. Whether children of slaves or of Ku Klux Klan members, whether victims of U.S.-trained assassination squads or children of wealth, they have not hidden behind barricades of anger or ivy-covered walls of privilege but have engaged as citizens in the healing of

America.

The new patriots are as different from each other as America itself. They include devout Christians, Jews, Baptists, and committed secular humanists; liberals and conservatives; blacks, whites, and Latinos; multimillionaires and impoverished immigrants; bank presidents, corporate executives, and inner city activists; policemen and "criminals." But as different as these Americans are, they have one thing in common. Like Patrick Henry, who declared that he was "not a Virginian but an American," the new patriots are transcending their loyalty to whichever Divided State they may once have belonged.

Notice, however, that these new patriots do not turn their backs on the Divided States to which they have previously belonged. On the contrary, they recognize the gifts of their respective States. Whether or not they believe in God, they recognize that they do believe in something higher than themselves—a vision of diversity joined into a greater whole. They pledge their allegiance to this vision—the United States of America—which beckons us to serve together a purpose higher than any of us could ever imagine, much less achieve, alone.

NOTES

This chapter could not have been written without the counsel and cooperation of countless colleagues who are active in the new "citizenship movement." I particularly want to thank my colleagues at the Rockefeller Foundation, the site leaders of The Common Enterprise, the staff of the National Civic League and the Alliance for National Renewal, the Civic Television Network, and the Civic Forum. This chapter also benefited from the advice of participants at several meetings, particularly "Revitalizing Citizenship" at the American Enterprise Institute (1994) and "The Citizenship Movement" at the Center for the Study of Community (1995).

1. Until 1892, the Pledge did not exist. It was written for part of a National School Celebration that year commemorating the 400th anniversary of Columbus's voyage to this continent, but it did not become official until an act of Congress made it part of our salute to the flag. It has been modified several times over the years—most recently in 1954, when anti-communist passions fueled a movement to add the words "under God." But even without the reference to divinity, the Pledge has been opposed by groups who felt the entire hand-over-the-heart exercise was chauvinistic. Its popularity has therefore waxed and waned along with public concepts of patriotism.

   The Pledge reiterates that we are committing ourselves "to the republic for which it [the flag] stands, one nation, under God, *indivisible*. . . ." We pledge allegiance to "the *flag* of the United States of America"—that is, to a symbol of the whole of which the states are but a part. The flag, like the "republic for which it stands," constantly changes. Every time a state is added to the union, a star is added. If read at this deeper level, the Pledge of Allegiance is not a call to mindless, flag-waving chauvinism. It is a call to the new patriotism.

2. *Roget's II: The New Thesaurus* (Boston, 1980).

3. George H. Gallup International Institute, November 1994: data from sampling of 1,205: margin of error plus or minus 3 percent. DYG, Inc., survey, February 1994. Confidence in religious leaders dropped from 57 to 40 percent between 1990 and 1994. Data provided by the National Civic League.

4. Peter Berger and Richard John Neuhaus, "To Empower People: The Role of Mediating Structures in Public Policy" (Washington, D.C., American Enterprise Institute).

5. DYG, Inc., survey, February 1994: figure 14, "Obstacles to a Healthy Community." Data provided by the National Civic League.

6. "How Everybody Lost in a Textbook Trial," *Woodrow Wilson Center Report*, vol. 5, no. 4, February 1994.

7. Cited by Kevin Phillips, *Arrogant Capital* (Boston, 1994), p. 133.

8. "US Likely to See More Gridlock," Knight-Ridder column by Robert Rankin and David Hess, *DC*, 11/9/94.

9. *NYT*, 10/10/94.

10. Associated Press national poll of 1,006 adults taken from October 28 to November 2, 1994, by ICR Survey Research Group of Media, PA, part of AUS Consultants.

11. The first definitions are from *Oxford English Dictionary;* the final definition is from *American Heritage Dictionary of the English Language.*

12. Lincoln, at a post-election celebration in Springfield, Illinois, November 20, 1860, cited in Cuomo and Holzer, *Lincoln on Democracy.*

13. It is worth noting here what it means to be "religious," in the original sense of the word. The origin of the word religion is *re* ("again") and *ligare* (to "bind," "bond," "bridge"). Being religious, in the deepest sense, means to join the different parts of life together in a sacred whole. To be religious means to connect ourselves, again and again, to what we have been disconnected from; to bond what has been broken apart; to bridge what has been torn asunder. Thus defined, spirituality is not a thorn in the side of democracy, it is a civic necessity. Robert A. Johnson, a Jungian analyst who has delved deeply into both myth and politics, writes: "The religious faculty is the art of taking the opposites and binding them back together again, surmounting the split that has been causing so much suffering. It helps us move from contradiction . . . to the realm of paradox, where we are able to entertain simultaneously two contradictory notions and give them equal dignity. Then, and only then, is there the possibility of grace, the spiritual experience of contradictions brought into a coherent whole." Robert A. Johnson, *Owning Your Own Shadow* (San Francisco, 1993), p. 85.

14. This often-cited statement by Jefferson was reprinted recently in the Civic Forum prospectus, October 1994.

15. Interview; All-America Cities Program, Oakland, CA, June 1994.

16. Lawrence Fuchs, *The American Kaleidoscope* (Hanover, NH, 1990), p. 277.

17. Cited in *DC*, 11/27/94.

18. Ellis Cose, *A Nation of Strangers* (New York, 1992) p. 11.
19. I am grateful to Matt Moseley for the research which produced this demographic data. If not otherwise indicated, it is based on Taeuber and Taeuber, *The Changing Population of the United States* (New York, 1958); Margo J. Anderson, *The American Census: A Social History* (New Haven, 1988); and Lawrence Fuchs, *The American Kaleidoscope*.
20. "Group Plans to Exploit G.O.P. Rise," *NYT*, 11/27/94.
21. These concepts are developed by Robert Fuller cited in McLaughlin and Davidson, *Spiritual Politics* (New York, 1994), p. 81.

CHILDREN'S BOOK

BY

PETER SÍS

AMY TAN

Required Reading and Other Dangerous Subjects

SEVERAL YEARS ago, I learned that I had passed a new literary milestone. I had made it to the Halls of Education under the rubric of "Multicultural Literature," also known in many schools as "Required Reading."

Thanks to this development, I now meet students at book signings who proudly tell me they're doing their essays, term papers, or master's theses on me. By that, they mean that they are analyzing not just my books but me—my grade-school achievements, youthful indiscretions, marital status, as well as the movies I watched as a child, the slings and arrows I suffered as a minority, and so forth—all of which, with the hindsight of classroom literary investigation, prove to contain many Chinese omens that made it inevitable that I would have become a writer.

I find these academic revelations quite strange, as if I were in a Dickensian story reading my obituary. Come to think of it, when I was a student, the only writers I analyzed had long since passed on to the Great Library in the Sky. They were dead and gone and therefore could not protest what I had said about them or their works. So if I wrote, "What Henry James really meant . . . ," there was no Henry James to say "You bloody fool, if that's what I meant, then that's what

I would have said."

I, however, have the distinct pleasure of hearing, while still very much alive, what I really meant when I wrote *The Joy Luck Club*. For example, one student discovered that my book is structured according to the four movements of a sonata: the proof lay in the fact that my parents had wanted me to become a concert pianist, as mentioned in my author's bio on the book jacket. I learned through another student, who culled in-depth biographical information from an authoritative source—*People* magazine—that my negative portrayals of husbands and fathers are based on my numerous bad experiences with men. I showed that essay to my husband, Lou, who has been my devoted companion for over twenty-five years.

As the recipient of such scholarly attention, I know I'm supposed to feel honored. Yet, in truth, I am more often embarrassed. It's as though I had eavesdropped on a party conversation and discovered that I was the subject of juicy gossip by a group of psychologists—or perhaps proctologists, depending on how in-depth and obsessive the analysis has become.

On one occasion, I read a master's thesis on feminist writings, which included examples from *The Joy Luck Club*. The student noted that I had often used the number four, something on the order of thirty-two or thirty-six times—in any case, a number divisible by four. Accordingly, she pointed out that there were four mothers, four daughters, four sections of the book, four stories per section. Furthermore, there were four sides to a mah jong table, four directions of the wind, four players. More importantly, she postulated, my use of the number four was a symbol for the four stages of psychological development, which corresponded in uncanny ways to the four stages of some type of Buddhist philosophy I had never heard of before. Extending this analysis even further, the student recalled that the story contained a character called Fourth Wife, symbolizing death, and a four-year-old girl with a feisty spirit, symbolizing regeneration. There was a four-year-old boy who drowns, and perhaps because his parents were Baptists, he symbolized rebirth through death. There was also a little girl who receives a scar on her neck at the age of four, who then loses her mother and her sense of self; she symbolized crisis.

In short, her literary sleuthing went on to reveal a mystical and rather Byzantine puzzle, which, once explained, proved to be completely brilliant and precisely logical. She wrote me a letter and asked if her analysis had been correct. How I longed to say "absolutely."

The truth is, I do indeed include images in my work, but I don't think of them as symbols, not in the Jungian sense. To me, symbols are stand-ins for abstract ideas. They belong to the High School of Hidden Meanings: vases symbolize female orifices, broken vases symbolize a loss of virginity and innocence. Heavy stuff. I prefer using images. My writing tends toward the Elementary School of Word Pictures: the accidental shattering of a vase in an empty room changes the emotions of a scene from serenity to uneasiness, perhaps even dread. The point is, if there are symbols in my work they exist largely by accident or through someone else's interpretive design. That is, they are more Freudian than Jungian, in the sense that what I intended and what I wrote are not what someone else says I meant. I don't *intend* to hide symbols at regular plot points. If I wrote of "an orange moon rising on a dark night," I would more likely ask myself later if the image was clichéd, not whether it was a symbol for the feminine force rising in anger, as one master's thesis postulated. To plant symbols like that, you need a plan, good organizational skills, and a prescient understanding of the story you are about to write. Sadly, I lack those traits. However, I do have a couple of Chinese and Western books on dream interpretation. Having two versions comes in handy. Say you dream that your teeth have fallen out. If one book gives you a bad interpretation, the other is often more optimistic.

All this is by way of saying that I don't claim my use of the number four to be a brilliant symbolic device. In fact, now that it's been pointed out to me in rather astonishing ways, I consider my *overuse* of the number four to be a flaw.

I'm not suggesting to you that I write my stories without any consideration of the words and images I include. I choose my words carefully, in fact, with much love and anguish. They are, each and every one, significant to me, by virtue of their meaning, their tone, their place in the sentence, their sound and rhythm in dialogue or narrative, their specific associations with something deeply personal and oftentimes secretly ironic in my life.

I know that in one instance I used the word "four" because its open vowel sounded softer and, thus, better to me than "three" or "five." On the other hand, the fact that I wrote that the mah jong table has four sides was a no-brainer; I have never seen a mah jong table with more or fewer than four sides.

As for the ages of the children in the book, I can say only that I was fond of the world at that age. Magic happened. Anything was possible; I didn't yet know what was not. And so at age four, when an auntie told me that my mother had eyes on the back of her head, I actually saw them peering out from underneath her permed hairdo. By the same childhood logic, insects talked to me, naked people danced underground, a marble of wax fell from my brain, into the tunnel of my ear, and onto the lap of my skirt. My imagination and reality were nearly the same thing. I believed what I heard. I then saw what I believed—which is not unlike what I, as a writer, would want readers to do when they read my stories. I have to make them believe the stories are true. And, in fact, some parts of them are—the character called Fourth Wife, for example. She is not called Fourth Wife for symbolic reasons. I wanted to pay homage to my real grandmother, who was indeed a fourth wife, who did kill herself as the result of her position in life, and who was the woman upon whom two of the stories were based.

Reviewers and students have enlightened me as to not only how I write, but *why* I write. Accordingly, I am driven to capture the immigrant experience, to demystify Chinese culture, to point out the differences between Chinese and American culture, even to pave the way for other Asian American writers.

If only I were that noble. The truth is, I write for myself. I write because I enjoy stories and make-believe, the power of words and the lovely peculiarities of language. I write because there is a lot I don't understand about life and death, myself and the world and the great in-between. I write because I am not the sort who can answer questions that ask true or false, yes or no, A, B, C, D, all of the above or none of the above. To me, the answers are irrelevant because the questions are wrong. I write to find the questions that I should ask. And for me, the stories are the possible answers, one story for each particular set of characters and circumstances.

I write for the same reasons I can't resist rubbing a numb spot on my kneecap where I tore my nerves. I like to poke at the numb spots of my memories, the secrets, lies, betrayals, contradictions, and losses. Underneath these old scars lies a painful kind of truth, fought for and prized because it belongs only to me. Rummaging through my memories, however, isn't like hitting rewind and replaying a video. I can change the past, make it better or worse. I can become the person who once wronged me. I can make that same person sorry. In effect, I write stories about life as I have misunderstood it. To be sure, it's a Chinese American life, but that's the only one I've had so far.

Contrary to what is assumed by some students, reporters, and community organizations wishing to bestow me with honors, I am not an expert on China, Chinese culture, mah jong, the psychology of mothers and daughters, generation gaps, immigration, illegal aliens, assimilation, acculturation, racial tension, Tiananmen Square, the Most Favored Nation trade agreements, human rights, Pacific Rim economics, the purported one million missing baby girls of China, the future of Hong Kong after 1997, or, I am sorry to say, Chinese cooking. Certainly I have personal opinions on many of these topics, especially on food, but by no means do my sentiments and my world of make-believe make me an expert.

And so I am alarmed when reviewers and educators assume that my very personal, specific, and fictional stories are meant to be representative down to the nth detail not just of Chinese Americans but, sometimes, of all Asian culture. Is Jane Smiley's *A Thousand Acres* supposed to be taken as representative of all of American culture? If so, in what ways? Are all American fathers tyrannical? Do all American sisters betray each other? Are all conscientious objectors flaky in love relationships? Why do readers and reviewers assume that a book with Chinese American characters can encompass all the demographics and personal histories of Chinese America?

My editor at Putnam's tells me that over the years she has received hundreds of permissions requests from publishers of college textbooks and multicultural anthologies, all of them wishing to reprint my work for educational purposes. One publisher wanted to include an excerpt from *The Joy Luck Club*, a scene in which a woman invites her non-Chinese boyfriend to her parents' house for dinner. The boyfriend brings a bottle of wine as a gift and commits a number of social gaffes at the dinner table. Students were supposed to read this excerpt, then answer the following question: "If you are invited to a Chinese family's house for dinner, should you bring a bottle of wine?"

I hear that my books and essays are now on the Required Reading lists for courses such as Ethnic Studies, Asian American Studies, Asian American Literature, Asian American History, Women's Literature, Feminist Studies, Feminist Writers of Color, and so forth. In many respects, I am proud to be on these lists. What writer wouldn't want her work to be read? I also take a certain perverse glee in imagining countless students, sleepless at three in the morning, trying to read *The Joy Luck Club* for the next day's midterm. Yet I'm also not altogether comfortable about my book's inclusion on Required Reading Lists— well, let me relate what I learned at a conference where I had been a guest speaker. At the end of my talk, an official from the California State Department of Education came up to me and said, "By the way, your books were recently approved for our state's multicultural recommended reading list for high schools."

I smiled gratefully but perhaps did not look sufficiently impressed, for she then went on to assure me, "Our criteria are very stringent. For a book to make it onto the list, it has to pass through a gauntlet of educators who must agree that the book under consideration will provide a positive and meaningful portrayal of the culture it represents."

Positive and meaningful portrayal. I was stunned by those words. I didn't know what to say to her, so I simply nodded, realizing that my books were contributing to dangerous changes in how people view literature. In fact, as I later discovered in talking to university friends, arguments fly back and forth in the halls of Ethnic Studies programs over which books are more valuable than others—all based on this so-called "stringent criteria concerning positive and meaningful portrayals of the cultures they are supposed to represent." Factions within minority groups have sprung up; the different sides throw sticks and stones at one another as they argue over what literature is supposed to represent, mean, and do. And a growing number of readers, educated readers, now choose fiction like cans of soup on a grocery shelf. If the book is labeled ethnic, it must contain specific nutritive ingredients: a descriptive narrative that provides lessons on culture, characters who serve up good role models, plots and conflicts that contain socially relevant themes and ideas, language that is wholesome in its political and ethnic correctness.

Recently, I talked to just such a reader, an agent—not my agent—but a young agent perhaps five years out of college. She said to me, "I love your books, they're so educational. What will your next book teach us? What's the lesson?" I told her, "I don't write books to teach people anything. If readers learn something, that's their doing, not mine."

The agent said, "Really? But don't you think you have a responsibility as a minority writer to teach the world about Chinese culture?"

Her comment reminded me that if you are a minority, your work may not be read in the same way that, say, Anne Tyler, John Updike, and Sue Grafton are read. Your novel might not be read as a good yarn, an enjoyable way to pass the time on the beach or a long airplane ride. No such frivol for your fiction, especially if it receives attention outside of your so-called ethnic community. And so, if you are a minority fiction writer, you should not presume that your work can reside in the larger world of imagination; it must be prepared to march into a territory of multicultural subject matters. You, the minority writer, must keep in mind that your work may be called upon to serve a higher purpose, that it might be inducted into a cultural lesson plan.

I know this is happening because I have received the student papers, the ones marked with an A for "excellent analysis of the differences between Chinese and American cultures." And it disturbs me, this trend in thinking, that there are those who think that literature has a predefined purpose. It terrifies me that well-meaning people are determining what literature must mean and say and do. And it infuriates me when people use the so-called authority of their race, gender, and class to stipulate who should write what and why. What exactly are their qualifications?

The prohibitions come in many forms. You can't write about lesbians unless you're a lesbian. You can't write about Native Americans unless you are at least twenty-five percent Native American and a registered member of your tribe. You can't write about African American or Asian American males unless the portrayals are positive. You can't write about the Hindus unless you are a member of the lower caste; you can't write about Latinos unless you still live in the barrio.

The mandates are just as strong. If you're gay, you must write about AIDS and explicit sex. If you are Asian American, you must write about modern, progressive characters, no harkening back to the bad old days. If you are African American, you must write about oppression and racism. And who are *you* to question these mandates if you're not a member of the particular minority group at issue?

I am beginning to hear this type of ethnic authority invoked more often these days. It's as though a new and more insidious form of censorship has crept into the fold, winning followers by wearing the cloak of good intentions and ethnic correctness. The leaders of the cause point to the negative and tiresome stereotypes found in the old literature—laborers, laundrymen, and peasants. They exhume the moral character of the author, citing, for example, that Hemingway was a misogynist and an anti-Semite. Shouldn't we stop reading works that have faulty ideas? Shouldn't we discourage writers who have faulty lifestyles?

The way I see it, the questions contain a faulty logic; they presume that what we read is what we condone. Then again, I'm one of those authors who have been told they have bad ideas. I'm the sort who would rather ask another question: can the ills of humanity be loaded up on a cart called literature and hauled away like so much trash? There are actually people who believe that the fictional world has the responsibility of righting the wrongs of the living world. They believe they can help eliminate racial stereotypes by censoring them in fiction.

If you disagree with such thinking, it's hard to parry with your own arguments. For one thing, any time you talk about ethnicity, you are in danger of tripping over terminology and landing in the battleground called racism. And in the unstable arena of ethnicity and race, there is no common language everyone agrees on. It's hard enough for me to determine what ethnic descriptors I use for myself. Do I refer to myself as a Chinese American writer, an ethnic writer, a minority writer, a Third World writer, a writer of color? From person to person, and particularly writer to writer, these terms carry different emotional and political weight.

Actually, if I had to give myself any sort of label, I would have to say I am an American writer. I am a Chinese by racial heritage. I am Chinese American by family and social upbringing. But I believe that what I write is American fiction by virtue of the fact that I was born in this country, that my linguistic intuitions are American English, that my literary sensibilities, assumptions, and obsessions are largely American. My characters may be largely Chinese American, but I think Chinese Americans are part of America.

As an aside, I must tell you that "writer of color" is an expression I personally dislike, since, in terms of color, Chinese people have always been referred to as yellow, the color associated with cowardice, jaundice, bananas, Ping the Duck, and the middle-class Marvin Gardens in Monopoly. I'd much prefer a term such as "colorful writers," which seems to refer more to the writing itself. Or how about "writers of different flavors?" Cuisine is probably a much closer indicator of differences in literary tastes than skin color. Writers of color is also an exclusionary term—you're not a member if your skin is too pale, and yet, perhaps the same issues face you as a writer if you're Armenian American or gay or lesbian or a woman. Whatever we are called, as the result of common experiences, both bad and humorous, we often have an affinity with one another. We are segregated in the same ways, placed on the same bookshelves and reading lists.

In fact, I wonder if literary segregation is one of the reasons why the cultural factions have arisen. We're pitted against one another. Consider book reviews. More often than not, if a book is by an Asian American writer, an Asian American is assigned by the newspaper or magazine editor to review it. On the surface, this seems to make sense: an Asian American reviewer may be more sensitive to the themes and meanings of the book—never mind that the reviewer is an academic in history, not a fiction writer, and possibly not even a fiction reader. But a reviewer who is thus qualified may dwell more on the historical relevance and accuracy of the book than on its literary merits—for instance, the language, the characters, the imagery, and story-telling qualities that seduce the reader into believing the tale is true. The review may be favorable, but it casts the book outside the realm of literature.

And woe are you if the Asian American reviewer champions both ethnic correctness and marginalism, believes your fiction should *not* depict violence, sexual abuse, mixed marriages, superstitions, Chinese as Christians, or mothers who speak in broken English.

If two or more books by Asian American writers are published in the same year, more likely than not, the book review editor will assign those books to be reviewed simultaneously by one reviewer. More likely than not the reviewer will compare the books, even though they may have nothing in common except for the fact that they are written by Asian Americans. Gus Lee's *China Boy* is compared to Gish Jen's *Typical American*, David Wong Louie's *Pangs of Love* is compared to Fae Myenne Ng's *Bone*, and so forth, and often through the tired and presbyopic, bifocal lens of two themes: immigration and assimilation. I remember what one reviewer at *The New York Times* had to say about my second book, *The Kitchen God's Wife*: "If one were to compare this book to *Shogun*, *The Good Earth*, works by Betty Bao Lord, Jade Snow Wong, Maxine Hong Kingston . . . ," and he continued further with his list of Asian names before concluding, " . . . it's been done before and better."

I found myself asking out loud "What's been done before? China? Suffering? Mothers? Death? Hope? Love? Pain?" I wasn't disagreeing with the reviewer's conclusion—those other books he cited might have been better—but what exactly was the basis of the comparison? And why was *Shogun* on the list?

I was talking about this mode of thinking to a friend of mine, a reporter who writes on literary matters and wears the badge of realist. He suggested that writers shouldn't complain. "Any attention is valuable," he said. "You can't demand attention. If you receive any, you should be grateful for what you get, good or bad, lumped together or not."

He went on, "The new writers would never get that kind of attention, unless they were grouped together for an angle. The media need an angle. Culture is the angle. A new wave in Asian American literature is the angle. They are not going to feature the writers separately as the next Joyce Carol Oates or the next Raymond Carver. They're not going to devote column inches to talking about the beauty of their prose, the cleverness of their characterization. That's not topical. That's not interesting."

He then cited the pragmatics of comparing books on their most superficial terms: "Readers do the same thing. They categorize and compare. They ask themselves, 'Do I want to read a mystery or a book about China? Old China or modern China? Mothers and daughters or warlords and evil empresses?' Consider yourself lucky," my friend advised.

I have been lucky in this regard. Nowadays my books are usually reviewed alone, and not alongside another book by an Asian American writer. More often than not, my books are reviewed by fiction writers who may or may not be Asian Americans. They are fiction writers, first and foremost. And thus they do discuss the relative literary merits and faults of my books and don't focus exclusively on

Chinese customs, superstitions, and positive role models. And for that I am enormously grateful.

But I worry about other writers yet to be published. I've been told that the success of my books has broken down barriers for other minority writers. Is that really true? Or do the successes of one writer sow land mines for another? Has the search for a media angle and an educational purpose created stiffer requirements on future writers? Are they now going to be subjected to a standard of representational realism? What will their responsibilities be? What, in fact, is any writer's responsibility?

The growing assumption is that the writer—any writer—by virtue of being published, has a responsibility to the reader. According to this ethic, the writer's musing, his or her imagination and delight in the world of make-believe, must be tamed and shaped by a higher consciousness of how the work will be interpreted—or rather, *mis*interpreted—by its readers. God forbid that a reader in some remote Texas hamlet might believe that all Chinese men have concubines, or that all Chinese mothers speak in broken English, or that all Chinese kids are chess grand masters.

I once met a professor of literature who taught at a school in Southern California. He told me he used my books in his literature class, but he made it a point to lambaste those passages that depict China as backward or unattractive. In other words, he objected to any descriptions that had to do with spitting, filth, poverty, or superstitions. I asked him if China in the 1930s and 1940s was free of these elements. And he said no, that the descriptions were true, but he still believed it was "the obligation of the writer of ethnic literature to create positive, progressive images."

I secretly shuddered and thought, Oh well, that's Southern California for you. But then, a short time later, I met a student from UC Berkeley, which is a school I also attended. The student was standing in a line during a book signing. When his turn came, he swaggered up to me, then took two steps back and said in a loud voice, "Don't you think you have the responsibility to write about Chinese men as positive role models?"

Mary Gaitskill, author of *Bad Behavior* and *Two Girls, Fat and Thin,* commented on this issue of the writer and his or her responsibilities. This is from her contributor's notes to a story, "The Girl on the Plane," which appeared in the 1993 edition of *Best American Short Stories*: ". . . I don't see how people can be responsible for their behavior if they are not responsible for their own thoughts and feelings. In my opinion, most of us have not been taught how to be responsible for our thoughts and feelings. I see this strongly in the widespread tendency to read books and stories as if they exist to confirm how we are supposed to be, think, and feel. I'm not talking about wacky political correctness, I'm talking mainstream. . . . Ladies and gentlemen, please. Stop asking 'What am I supposed to feel?' Why would an adult look to me or another writer to tell him or her what to feel? You're not *supposed* to feel anything. You feel what you feel. Where you go with it is your responsibility. If a writer chooses to aggressively let you know what he or she feels, where you go with it is still your responsibility."

I suppose that if writers were responsible for people's thoughts and for creating positive role models, we would then be in the business of writing propaganda, not art as fiction. Fiction makes you think. Propaganda tells you how to think; it's the mindset of those who led the Cultural Revolution in China.

Yet there are folks who believe that's what fiction by minority writers should do: tell people what to think. These writers believe, for example, that if you're Asian American, you should write about contemporary Asian Americans—none of that old China stuff—and that your work should be exclusively for Asian Americans and not a mainstream audience. If your work is inaccessible to white readers, that is proof that it is authentic. If it is read by white people, then that is proof that the work is fake, a sellout, and hence the writer is to be treated as a traitor, publicly branded and condemned. While the numbers within this faction are small, their influence in academia and the media is substantial. They shout for attention and they receive it.

A couple of years ago, I was at a conference on Asian Americans and the arts. A professor of literature spoke passionately into the microphone about the importance, the necessity of "Asian Americans maintaining our marginalism." She rallied the crowd to believe it was the responsibility of Asian American writers and artists to remain apart from the mainstream. She believed in a Marxist model of thinking for minorities, that the dominant class was the enemy and minorities should work separately from them as part of the struggle. "There is strength in marginalism," she shouted.

To me, that kind of thinking is frightening, a form of literary fascism. It is completely antithetical to why I write, which is to express myself freely in whatever direction or form I wish. I can't imagine being a writer and having others dictate to me what I should write, why I should write, and who I should write for. And this is the real reason I consider myself an American writer: I have the freedom to write whatever I want. I claim that freedom.

I've been trying to understand why these factions sprang up in the first place. I suspect that they have their origins in bitterness, anger, and frustration in being excluded. I've experienced those same feelings in my life, growing up Chinese American in a white community. As a teenager, I suspected the real reason I was never asked to dance had to do with my being Chinese rather than, say, my nerdiness. As a cynical college student, I realized my forefathers never ate turkey, never fell down chimneys dressed in red costumes. In my twenties, I joined various Pacific Asian groups and became an activist for multicultural training programs for special educators.

If not for a few circumstances that led to where I am today, would I have become one of those activists for ethnically correct literature? If I hadn't found my voice in a published book, would I too have shouted from a podium that there is strength in marginalism? If I had written book after book, starting in the seventies, and none of them had been published or reviewed, would I also have been tempted to feel there was a conspiracy going on in the publishing industry? Would I have believed that those Asian Americans who did get published and reviewed had sold their souls and were serving up a literary version of chop suey for American palates?

As I thought about those questions, I remembered when I was an English major in 1970 (at a time, by the way, when there were fewer than 450,000 Chinese Americans in all the United States, including Hawaii, compared to 7.2 million today). In the American literature classes I took, I read Hemingway, Faulkner, Fitzgerald, Sinclair Lewis, Theodore Dreiser—the usual assortment of dead white males. It didn't bother me—or, rather, I didn't question that it could be any other way. In fact, during those years that I was an English major, the only female novelist I read was Virginia Woolf; I had originally thought there was another, Evelyn Waugh (those Brits have peculiar ways of addressing men). The only minority writers I read were in a class I took called Black Literature, which is where I read Richard Wright, James Baldwin, Ralph Ellison—but again no books by women. I didn't even consider that there was such a thing as a book by an Asian American woman; Maxine Hong Kingston's book *Woman Warrior* didn't come out until 1976.

Back in my college days of the early seventies, we hadn't yet discovered political correctness. But when I read the books on Required Reading lists—*An American Tragedy, The Grapes of Wrath, Babbitt, Tender Is the Night*—I too was required to look at character flaws as symbols of social ills. Soon I became adept at writing papers that alluded to the trickier symbols and more subtle themes that I knew would please my professors. I could tell by the tone of their lectures which books they admired, which ones we had to read so that, should we one day become literary critics, we would know how to properly heap scorn. And thus I would wade through each semester's stack of required reading, pen and paper at hand, ready to catch symbols and social themes with much the same focus as a gardener searching for weeds, snails, and leaf rot. When I completed my literature requirements in 1971, I stopped reading fiction. What I had once loved I no longer enjoyed.

I didn't resume reading fiction on a regular basis until 1985. I don't think it was coincidence that what I chose to read was largely stories by women writers: Flannery O'Connor, Isabel Allende, Louise Erdrich, Eudora Welty, Laurie Colwin, Alice Adams, Amy Hempel, Alice Walker, Lorrie Moore, Anne Tyler, Alice Munro, Harriet Doerr, and Molly Giles. I wasn't trying to be a literary chauvinist. I also read works by García Márquez, Raymond Carver, David Leavitt, Tobias Wolff, Richard Ford. But mostly I read fiction by women, simply because I had so rarely read a novel by a woman in my adult years, and I found I enjoyed their sensibilities, their voices, and what they had to say about the world. I was feeling again the thrill I had as a child, choosing my own books, falling in love with characters, reading stories because I couldn't stop myself. In fact, I kept reading day and night until I couldn't stop myself from *writing*.

When I was first published in 1989 at the age of thirty-seven, interviewers asked me why I waited so long to write fiction. I could only answer, "It never occurred to me that I could." By that, I didn't mean I lacked the desire. I thought I lacked the qualifications: a disposition to plant tricky symbols in carefully tilled rows of sentences. Expertise on white whales and white males. A state of being known as dead. The idea of my becoming a published contemporary fiction writer was as ludicrous as, say, my wearing a dominatrix costume while singing rock and roll on stage at the Los Angeles Palladium with Bruce Springsteen— which, by the way, I recently did. Suffice it to say, little of my educational past encouraged me to be a writer. If anything, it discouraged me.

This short history of my educational background is saying by way of example that minorities and women were largely ignored in the literature curriculum until a couple of decades ago. And so I can readily see the reasons professors and students campaigned for the inclusion of Ethnic Studies programs. They pointed out how minorities had been "marginalized"—excluded as bonafide Americans or relegated to the sidebars of history books, to footnotes in social and psychological issues. To get rid of the narrow slant in how minorities were treated in the curriculum, the formerly Excluded We had to create a separate department, separate but as equal as we could make it. At last we had stories and histories of Asian Americans written by Asian Americans, taught by Asian Americans, and read by Asian American students. At last we had a history that went beyond the railroads and the laundries of the Gold Rush days. But because we had so few resources, we borrowed from story to account for history. We turned to fiction, letting an imaginary world represent the real one.

As a result, cultural sensitivity became a bristling issue, prickling some to hypersensitivity. During the same period, American demographics changed dramatically. I remember a time when I was the only Chinese person to ever set foot in certain towns. I would wager that today the average American knows on a first-name basis at least one Asian American—through work, school, their child's daycare, their athletic club, their neighborhood store, their church, or what have you. In other words, times have changed.

Unfortunately, in some circles these notions of literary -isms—separatism, multiculturalism, marginalism—are territories that must be vigilantly defended. And thus minority writers are often asked, "Are you one of them or one of us?"—meaning we can't be both. We're asked, "Are you writing American literature or Asian American literature?"—meaning one is not the other. "Are you writing for Asian Americans or the mainstream?"—meaning one necessarily excludes the other. And those of us (including Bharati Mukherjee, Maxine Hong Kingston, and myself) who say we are American writers have been censured by the separatists, reviled at podiums, and denounced with expletives in the student press.

In the past, I've tried to ignore the potshots. A *Washington Post* reporter once asked me what I thought of another Asian American writer calling me something on the order of "a running dog whore sucking on the tit of imperialist white pigs."

"Well," I said, "you can't please everyone, can you?" I went on to point out that readers are free to interpret what they will or want out of a book, and they are free to appreciate or not appreciate what they've interpreted. Besides, reacting to your critics makes a writer look defensive, petulant, and like an all-round bad sport.

But lately I've started thinking it's wrong to take such a laissez-faire attitude. Lately I've come to think I must say something not so much to defend myself and my work but to express my hopes for American literature, what it has the possibility of becoming in the twenty-first century—that is, a truly American literature, democratic in the way it includes many colorful voices.

Until recently, I didn't think it was important for writers to express their private intentions in order for their work to be appreciated. My domain is fiction, and I believed the analysis of my intentions belonged behind the closed doors of literature classes. But I've come to realize that the study of literature does have its effect on how books are being read, and thus on what might be read, published, and written in the future. For that reason, I do believe writers today must talk about their intentions—if anything, to serve as an antidote to what others define as to what our intentions should be.

For the record, I don't write to dig a hole and fill it with symbols that stand for general ideas. I don't write stories as ethnic themes. I don't write to represent life in general. And I certainly don't write because I have answers. If I knew everything there is to know about mothers and daughters, Chinese and Americans, I wouldn't have any stories left to imagine. If I had to write about only positive role models, I wouldn't have enough imagination left to finish the first story. If I knew what to do about immigration, I would be a sociologist or a politician, and not a long-winded storyteller.

So why do I write?

Because my childhood disturbed me, pained me, made me ask foolish questions. And the questions still echo. Why does my mother always talk about killing herself? Why did my father and brother have to die? If I die, can I be reborn into a happy family? Those early obsessions led to a belief that writing could be my salvation, providing me with the sort of freedom and danger, satisfaction and discomfort, truth and contradiction I can't find in anything else in life.

I write stories because I still have questions about life, not answers. I believe life is mysterious and not dissectable. What is love? What is hope? How do you know they exist? How do you know when they're gone?

I write because oftentimes I can't express myself any other way, and I think I'll explode if I don't find the words. Sad, happy, scared, angry—those words aren't adequate. I can't paraphrase or give succinct morals about love and hope, pain and loss. I have to use a mental long-hand, ponder and work it out in the form of a story that is revised over and over again, twenty times, until it feels true.

I write for very much the same reasons I read: to startle my mind, to churn my heart, to tingle my spine, to knock the blinders off my eyes and allow me to see beyond the pale. I write for the specific and unique ways that words can evoke emotions and images and thus give both pain and pleasure, wonder and confirmation about what it means to be alive. Fiction is my intimate companion and confidante for life.

I write because I have been in love with words since I was a child. I hoarded words from the thesaurus and the dictionary as though they were magical gems and sharp glass, good medicine and deadly poison. I used metaphors before I ever knew what the word metaphor meant. I played with them as images, and, like dreams, they were the secret passageways that took me to hidden rooms, to the closed-off places of my heart and memory, to a make-believe world where childhood hopes became wishes come true.

I played with imagined life the way young girls played with their Barbies, the way young boys played with their penises—with constancy and fervor. I dressed it up, changed it a dozen times, manipulated it, tugged at it, wondered if it would enlarge and pulsate until others noticed it too. I thought of it as a forbidden joy, a secret sin, an incorrigible vice.

I write to rediscover the past for myself. I don't write to change the future for others. And if others are moved by my work—if they love their mothers more, scold their daughters less, or divorce their husbands who were not positive role models—I'm often surprised, usually grateful to hear from kind readers. But I don't take either credit or blame for changing their lives for better or for worse.

I write because it is the ultimate freedom of expression. And for that reason it is also as scary as skiing down a glacier, as thrilling as singing in a rock and roll band, as dangerous as falling on my face doing both.

Writing, for me, is an act of faith, a hope that I will discover what I mean by truth. But I don't know what that will be until I finish. I can't determine it ahead of time. And more often than not I can't summarize what it is I've discovered. It's simply a feeling. The feeling is the entire story. To paraphrase the feeling or to analyze the story reduces the feeling for me.

I also think of reading as an act of faith, a hope I will discover something remarkable about ordinary life, about myself. And if the writer and the reader discover the same thing, if they have that connection, the act of faith has resulted in an act of magic. To me, that's the mystery and the wonder of both life and fiction—the connection between two unique individuals who discover in the end that they are more the same than they are different.

And if that doesn't happen, it's nobody's fault. There are still plenty of other books on the shelf. Choose what you like.

PHILLIP LOPATE

The Moody Traveler

TRAVELING ALONE has its pluses: you can go
where you want when you want, and you are spared that runaway irritation that
comes of suddenly spotting all the little flaws in your companion (who alone
seems to be detaining you from perfect enjoyment) and the tension of having to
keep that knowledge secret. However, the minus is that you will have no one to
blame but yourself for the occasional rotten mood. The ecstasies and lone
epiphanies of the morning museum eventually evaporate, and by late afternoon,
after a mediocre overpriced lunch has made you sluggish, you are ready to turn
the big guns on yourself. To travel is to brood, and especially if you are your sole
company. I would go so far as to recommend traveling alone as an excellent way
of catching up with all the poor opinions of yourself that you may have had to
suppress during the busy, camouflaging work-year, when it is necessary to
appear a self-approving, winning member of society.

I remember one such afternoon in beautiful Florence when the charm I
derived from my personality was at a low point. I had mapped out my agenda
for a visit to the nearby hill town of Fiesole. Though I could have taken the
excursion bus near my hotel, I commanded myself to hike, ostensibly because it

was good exercise, and because you see so much more on foot, but in actuality, I realize now, to punish myself.

As I slogged uphill past "rows of cypresses and sumptuous villas" (Michelin guide), my mind was so filled with worthless thoughts which broke off and told me so little—that I had the impression not of a walk through a real landscape but of one continuous spiteful déjà vu. It was a playback of all those times I had walked enviously and stupidly through the world of rich houses where I didn't belong. Nothing less than owning a villa, *any* villa, on this Italian hill would satisfy me. Yet I saw so little of the actual residences I coveted, their gardens or marble sculptures or whatever I was supposed to look at, that even in my surly mood this envy struck me as comic. Envy for a landscape I took so little trouble to observe? Perhaps we only envy that which we look at superficially; and a deeper look would take care of our urge for possession? Nah. In any case, I kept walking.

I arrived at a flat village square cut into the hill, where tourist buses were parked in the afternoon heat. Fiesole. Was it sunny? Clouded over? I wasn't interested enough to notice. I headed for a café that seemed to exist on the trade of tourists waiting for their bus driver to return from who knows where and start his engine. I sat down at the nickel-plated soda fountain, with the momentarily satisfied sense of having stumbled on a "find." Not that the stopover was attractive, but it was at least an oasis of decrepitude: there were dusty cutout doll books and movie magazines, and a faded Italian novelization of Erich Segal's *Love Story*. I ordered a Campari, hoping for a mindless respite. Yet, just as soon as I had drained it, a spasm of restlessness overcame me and I paid and walked out.

By now I was thoroughly fed up with my impatience. I was determined to slow down and practice "the discipline of seeing." It was a sometime conviction of mine that, wherever one found oneself, the world was rich enough to yield enjoyment if one but paid close attention to the details. Or, as John Cage once said, when something bores you, keep looking at it and after a while you will find it intriguing. Inside, however, I rebelled against this notion, which struck me as forced quietism—an aestheticizing trick to bring about the opposite of what one knows to be true. The day is boring, horrible? Very well, that's the card I've been dealt. Let's not pretend it's any better.

I was still arguing these two positions when I sat down on a bench overlooking what I knew most people would think a magnificent vista. All of the Arno Valley and Florence were stretched before us. The city fathers had wisely provided benches. Not only was this undeniably and obviously a magnificent vista, but it was an "officially recognized" magnificent vista, even more annoying. But then, what *had* escaped the tourist industry's exploitive eye in Italy? Where could one find any beauty in this country that was fresh and unframed?

This line of thinking soon struck me as foolish petulance. The truth is I loved Italy, so what was I whining about?

I literally forced myself to concentrate on the Italian family a few benches over. The son was leaning semidangerously over the hilltop. That could be interesting. But then he sat down next to his father, who was cutting an orange rind circularly with a fruit knife. I wondered if this orange paring was an Old World custom. (Vapid anthropologizing to replace self-ennui.) The mother was taking thick sandwiches out of a plastic bag and handing them all around. They seemed a big, warm, friendly family—two daughters, one son, a father, a mother— speaking casually to each other, eating their picnic lunch, playing with the dog.

To fathom the secret of that Italian familial harmony, I watched them covertly for ten minutes, dividing my attention between their interactions and the landscape below, and came to the conclusion that they weren't as warm as I had originally given them credit for. They simply ate a great deal. The more I watched them, the more it dawned on me that there was absolutely nothing exceptional about them. That in itself was unusual. Most families yield up fairly rich pathologies, but this one did not interest me in any conceivable way. My hypothesis about steady attention to detail was being contradicted.

At about this time an elderly Italian man, tall, angular, bald, toothless save for one top incisor, looking in his mid-seventies—about the age of my father, in fact—came up and asked with gestures if he could sit on my bench. This seemed a little odd, as there was another bench completely unoccupied, but who was I to deny a fellowman my company if he thought he could reap some nourishment therefrom? Had I not been complaining of the burden of my solitude? Perhaps this old guy would amuse me or turn into a *vivid anecdotal experience*, the goal of all tourists at loose ends.

"What is your name?" he asked me in halting English. I told him. "And yours?" Nicola. He tried out his few English questions on me, I answered him in my limited Italian. It was the sort of conversation one has on the road often, and which seems to exist in order to prove that the stiff dialogues of phrase books are, in fact, the height of naturalism. The old man began to talk about his work in a garage (I think he said he was a retired mechanic) and to complain that now he had nothing to do. He told me about his sons, his wife, his vineyard. These Italians, I reflected, are unquenchably sociable, they love to chatter. True, I had my doubts that this was going to lead to a vivid anecdotal experience, and was already feeling bored, since I understood only one out of every three sentences, but I congratulated myself on being such a good and patient listener. The man is obviously lonely, I thought; he reminds me of the aged pensioner in De Sica's *Umberto D*; perhaps I can reap from him some necessary lesson in humility and human dignity. Meanwhile, he was talking my ear off in Italian, and I was nodding and pursuing some interior reverie about how sad it is that society is so afraid of the old, how wrong that we back off so squeamishly from them, and he had just gotten to the part where he told me his wife had died when he seized my hand in an iron grip.

At first I did nothing, pretending it was a sort of international brotherhood handshake; but then I tried to pull away, and discovered that the old man was not letting go. I stared at his frayed white shirt, buttoned to the top, pulled taut by his chest; he was like a wooden plank, not a scrap of fat on him. I looked around for help to the picnicking family, but they had apparently wandered off without my noticing. Now he grinned in what seemed a possibly rather lecherous manner—at the same time trying to reassure me that he was not going to hurt me. He only wanted to hold my hand. So we sat there, my hand sweating in his. He had very large brown fingers, liver-spotted around the webs.

I immediately recalled a strange incident that had once happened to my sister. She had entered a subway car in New York and sat down next to a blind man. He had a braille book open in his lap. She stared without embarrassment at his face, which was lined, blotched as if from poison ivy. There was no reason to assume he felt her interest. It so happens that my sister is very pretty, but how could the blind man know that? Suddenly he took hold of her arm. She thought he wanted her to help guide him out of the train or across the platform, and began to explain that it wasn't her stop yet, but he paid no attention. She felt his hand working down her arm until it had captured her hand. He began squeezing each of her fingers separately, all the while kneading her palm. She could not take her eyes off their two hands, like starfish swimming locked together. She felt she should scream, but no sound came out; she just sat there, paralyzed, ashamed and, my sister admitted candidly, fascinated. "This man was an artist of hands," she recalled. He had supreme tactile sensitivity. Finally his grip loosened, he closed his eyes, and she looked down at his brown pants, which were stained near the fly. It outraged her that he might ride the subways daily and molest women and they would probably say nothing, just because he was blind.

Anyhow, this old toothless Italian next to me was by no stretch of the imagination an artist of hands. He simply had a very powerful grip. I began to speculate about his secret life, in and around the good family man and laborer, of chance pickups. I didn't even know if he was gay necessarily, or if he was so starved for human touch, the memory of young flesh, that it didn't matter which sex he accosted. How many tourists before me had he done this with? Were we all Americans? I wondered. If he did try any funny stuff, I was sure I could hold him off. But all he seemed to be doing so far was holding my hand and smiling—every so often he would wriggle the wrist a little in the air and grin at me, as if we were both relaxing from a good arm-wrestle.

By this time other tourists had joined us on the hilltop (to my relief) and were consuming the landscape. I too looked down at the vista, since I had nothing better to do and was tired of trying to figure out the old man's game. Now the shifting pattern of light over the valley—a dusky evening light that brought out the muted pinks, the muddy browns, the raked greens of cultivated countryside and, in the distance, Florence, all salmon and white walls—seemed to me extremely fetching. For the first time all day, I was able to enjoy the physical world around me. Were I given to looking on the bright side, or religious allegories, or megalomania, I might say that the old man was an angel sent down by God to handcuff me to one spot and force me to attend the earth with pleasure.

I suppose part of what kept me from retrieving my hand was the flattering knowledge that *someone* at least desired me, needed me at that moment, in this place through which I had taken it upon myself to travel alone. For the longest while, neither of us said anything. Then he got up, gave me a courtly bow, muttered "*Grazie*" in a hoarse, dry voice, and strode off. Watching his bald brown head and stiff back recede, I laughed disbelievingly at what had just happened. The weirdness of it had driven away my black mood, and I kept laughing all the way home on the tourist bus. For those who do not like happy endings, my apologies.

ROSEMARY WELLS

THE ISLAND LIGHT

from *Voyage to the Bunny Planet*

Felix was sick in front of the whole art class.

The nurse made him a cup of tea and called home.
Nobody answered the phone.
Felix burned his tongue on the tea.

That afternoon the doctor gave Felix medicine
that tasted like gasoline.
Felix's mother and the nurse had to hold him
down for a shot.

Later Felix was accidentally soaked by an icy shower.

Felix's father was busy in the cellar with the boiler.
Felix's mother was busy finding a plumber.
Both forgot to kiss him good night.

Felix needs a visit to the Bunny Planet.

Far beyond the moon and stars,
Twenty light-years south of Mars,
Spins the gentle Bunny Planet
And the Bunny Queen is Janet.

"Felix," Janet says. "Come in.
Here's the day that should have been."

The mailboat comes at six o'clock.
I walk my father to the dock.

The boat brings apples, milk, and flour,
And sails back home within the hour.

A squall is stirring up the sky.
Our lighthouse home is warm and dry.

The light was built in nineteen-ten.
It's had six keepers here since then.

We're wet and salty, but who cares?
Our sweaters dry on kitchen chairs.

We mix an apple pancake batter,
Singing while the shutters clatter.

The night wind howls. The rain leaks in.
After supper we play gin.

155

Our sweaters steam. The fire crackles.
The ocean swells and lifts its hackles.

We split a piece of gingerbread
And play another round in bed.

Outside the sea enfolds the sand.
Inside I hold my father's hand.

Felix wakes at midnight.
Out his bedroom window he sees the Bunny Planet
near the Milky Way in the summer sky.
"It was there all along!" says Felix.

JOHN EGERTON

John Lewis

from *A Mind to Stay Here:*
Profiles from the South

Some men see things as they are and say why. I dream things
that never were and say why not.

GEORGE BERNARD Shaw wrote that, and Robert
F. Kennedy was making it the theme of his campaign for the Presidency when he
was killed. It is a nice statement, full of idealism and hope. It appeals to a lot of
people who believe in the principles and promises of American democracy—and
who have had few personal experiences to shake that belief. For many people
whose homes have been shattered, whose churches have been burned, whose
votes have been stolen, whose heads have been broken—for many of America's
disinherited—dreams are nightmares, dreaded, dangerous, destructive things. For
those people, hope is a luxury. The reality is hopelessness and despair and rage.

But then there are people like John Lewis. He is a black Southerner, thirty
years old. He has fought for justice for black people ever since he got out of high
school in Pike County, Alabama, in 1957. He has been to jail forty times. He has
been beaten unconscious in the streets.

George Bernard Shaw's idealistic credo hangs over the sofa in John Lewis's living room. It is an affirmation of hope that speaks to him. He likes it, and he believes deeply in the spirit of it. Dreaming things that never were and saying why not is pretty much what John Lewis has been doing for the past decade.

Lewis is an enigma. I heard a man who has known him for several years ask, "How could anybody who's been through what that guy's been through really be that free of bitterness and hate?" It's a good question. He has made a habit of doing unpopular things because he thought they were right, and he has paid a heavy price for it. Nonviolence brought down the wrath of white supremacy on his head—and later, it cost him his leadership role in the student wing of the civil-rights movement. He led marches and demonstrations when some of the most radical strategists of the Movement begged him to hold off—and he compromised when some of the same people counseled him to stand his ground. He followed his own social interpretation of the Gospel and left his church for the streets—just when a lot of "liberal" churchmen were hiding behind their stained glass windows. After both religion and politics had betrayed the black American masses, Lewis was able to bring innocent enthusiasm to a political cause. He has been denounced as a dangerous radical by the white Establishment—and some black radicals have written him off as not "black" enough, or not violent enough.

And John Lewis goes on being who he is—a gentle man, quiet and shy, as consistent and as persistent in his pursuit of justice for Negroes and the poor as he ever was. He is now director of the Voter Education Project of the Southern Regional Council in Atlanta. Four years ago, after he had lost the chairmanship of the Student Nonviolent Coordinating Committee to Stokely Carmichael, Lewis went to New York to work for the Field Foundation. He lasted fourteen months, and then gave it up and went South again—to stay.

The civil-rights movement led Lewis into the ministry—and later out of it. He was born in 1940, six miles from Troy, Alabama, on a small farm his father rented. John was the third of ten children. In 1944 his father bought 100 acres of land in Pike County for $300, and it took the whole family to scrape out a living from the cotton, peanuts, and corn they grew on it. School for them was a luxury—neither of his parents was able to go beyond the ninth grade—and there were times when John had to hide under the house and wait for the school bus, to keep from having to go to the fields.

As a teenager, one of his responsibilities was taking care of the chickens. "I fell in love with them," he recalls. "They were so innocent. I named them, talked to them, assigned them to coops and guided them in every night, and when one of them died, I preached his funeral and then buried him. I also protested whenever one of them was killed for food. I refused to eat." He smiled at the recollection.

"I guess that was my first protest demonstration."

John wanted to be a minister, and that pleased his good Baptist parents, because there were no preachers in the family. But his interest in the ministry did not fit any traditional pattern. In Montgomery, fifty miles from his home, black people led by the Rev. Martin Luther King, Jr., were boycotting the city buses, and Lewis was impressed: "It had a tremendous impact on me. I had come to resent segregation and discrimination at an early age. We had the poor schools, the run-down school buses, the unpaved roads; and I saw that those were penalties imposed on us because of race. So race was closely tied to my decision to be a minister. I thought religion could be something meaningful, and I wanted to use the emotional energy of the black church to end segregation and gain freedom for black people." He was ordained in 1956, the year before he graduated from high school.

Morehouse was where he wanted to go to college, but he didn't have the money. His mother worked for a white Southern Baptist, and one day she brought home a magazine that had something in it about the American Baptist Theological Seminary in Nashville. ABTS was a small institution owned jointly by the National Baptist Convention (Negro) and the Southern Baptist Convention (white), with the latter group providing most of the support—a kind of insurance against desegregation. Lewis wrote for an application, filled it out, and was accepted. He got a job as a dishwasher in the school kitchen to pay his room and board.

For the first couple of years, John didn't venture far from the seminary campus, but his attitudes about the organized church and the civil-rights movement continued to change. "My first semester I was in church every Sunday," he says, "but by the second semester I had begun to drift away. It was a period of real doubt and change for me. I started to question for the first time the ritual, the ceremony, the creeds and beliefs of the church, and I began to identify more and more with the social aspects of Jesus' life." He also formed close friendships with two fellows students at the seminary who later were active with him in the civil-rights struggle—Bernard Lafayette and James Bevel.

When he went home for Christmas his freshman year, Lewis made application to enter Troy State College as a transfer student, but his application was ignored. The Montgomery Improvement Association, headed by Martin Luther King, wanted to pursue the application in court, and John later met with King, Ralph Abernathy, and Fred Gray to discuss it, but his parents were afraid of the possible repercussions, so the matter was dropped. John also tried to organize a student chapter of the NAACP at the seminary, but the president feared losing Southern

Baptist support, and once again he acquiesced.

By the fall of 1959, the South was beginning to feel the pinch of racial protest. School desegregation was the big issue—highlighted by the Little Rock episode—but other grievances were growing, and Nashville was a fertile field for some of them. Nashville's Negro colleges and churches had in their ranks a good-ly number of black ministers, educators, and students who became prominent in civil rights during the early 1960s. Although they and the black lawyers and the assortment of whites allied to the cause never joined together in any single orga-nization, the city had a cadre of black leaders as diverse and talented as any city in the South. The NAACP, the new Southern Christian Leadership Conference headed by Dr. King, the Southern Regional Council, and other civil-rights groups had strong chapters there, and students from the city's colleges and universities were meeting and organizing before Atlanta and other cities got into the act. Young people such as Lewis, Bevel, Lafayette, the Rev. James Lawson, Diane Nash, and Marion Barry made the Nashville movement prominent as a center of young black protest.

Lawson, a Methodist minister and a student at the Vanderbilt Divinity School, conducted workshops in nonviolence for Nashville's SCLC chapter in the fall of 1959, and most of his students were young people from the colleges. Lawson lec-tured them on the philosophy, history, and discipline of nonviolence, and in November they staged the first sit-in in the South—three months before students in Greensboro, North Carolina, got national publicity using the same tactics. The Nashville sit-in was a test to establish the fact that lunch counters in the down-town stores wouldn't serve Negroes. The students requested service, were refused, and left. It all happened almost without notice, but it was the beginning, and after that there was no turning back. Lawson was later expelled from Vanderbilt Divinity School for leading the sit-ins.

The next month, on their way home for Christmas, Lewis and Lafayette board-ed a bus for Birmingham, and took the front seat. The driver told them to move but they refused, and they rode all the way to Birmingham sitting there—two black youngsters full of pride and exhilaration at what they sensed was happen-ing to them and the movement and the South. Lewis recalls the high spirits of those early months:

> *It was an exciting time, that time of beginning. Everything*
> *was so simple, and we were so clear about where we were*
> *going. It was just right. It was nonviolent, and interracial, and*
> *daring, and religious. It was like a holy war, a crusade, and we*

saw the movement rising across the South, we saw change com-
ing, and we were helping to bring it about. We were volunteers
committed to the philosophy of nonviolence, in keeping with the
New Testament and the Christian faith. My motivation came
from religious conviction—segregation was immoral, illegal,
and unchristian, and it had to be destroyed. You felt you had to
be consistent with the truth, be faithful unto death, and there
was integrity in that, and peace. Later, when we were charged
with disorderly conduct and trespassing, we believed that a
positive peace would come out of conflict, that it was a good
thing to bring a lot of dirt and filth and trouble to the surface
so it could be expelled.

Through the first six months of 1960, the sit-ins grew in size and frequency. They were marked by victories and setbacks, new allies and new enemies, capitulations and hold-outs, occasional violence and frequent arrest. Lewis was arrested for the first time in February:

We had been marching from Kelly Miller Smith's First
Baptist Church, sometimes 200 or 300 of us at a time, but that
day there were only thirty or so. Will Campbell told us that the
merchants had been to the mayor and the police, and that we
would surely be arrested if we marched. There was a real
debate among the older leaders. Most of them didn't want us to
go, but we went anyway. We had been well prepared in nonvio-
lence—don't strike back, be polite, smile, be friendly, remember
the teachings of Jesus, Gandhi, Martin Luther King—so we
went. All of us were arrested, and we spent the day in jail. We
went in high spirits, singing—we knew we were right. Bail
money was sent in from the National Student Association, and
that was the start of the legal end of things—arrests, bail, tri-
als, appeals, lawyers.

For Lewis, that process would be repeated many times.

In April, SCLC called a meeting in Raleigh for leaders of the sit-in movement, and students came from all over the South. King was there, and Ralph Abernathy, and Ella Baker, then the executive director of SCLC. "Some people wanted to form a student wing of SCLC," Lewis recalls,

> *but the students wanted an independent organization. We formed a temporary independent group, with Marion Barry as chairman, and that was the beginning of the Student Nonviolent Coordinating Committee. The Atlanta and Nashville students were at odds with each other over where to put the headquarters. We had the best organized, best disciplined group, but they had the money, and SCLC offered to provide space, so the headquarters was set up in Atlanta, but we had the chairman in Nashville, and our student movement there remained the strongest for a long time.*

Lewis says that Ella Baker, "perhaps more than any other person, was responsible for making SNCC what it became. She was sort of the mother of SNCC. She's a great lady."

With representatives from all the major civil-rights organizations there as observers, SNCC met in Atlanta the following October and formed a permanent organization. Barry was installed as chairman, and Diane Nash represented the Nashville chapter on the coordinating committee. More demonstrations followed in the winter and spring of 1961.

Then came the Freedom Rides. The Congress on Racial Equality sent out a call for volunteers to test a recent Supreme Court decision outlawing discrimination in interstate travel, and Lewis applied to go. After an orientation in Washington, he and twelve others set out by bus on two separate itineraries to New Orleans, with layovers and rallies planned at several places along the way. Lewis and his group rode buses through Virginia and North Carolina without encountering any serious incidents, but at Rock Hill, South Carolina, as they started toward the white waiting room, John was attacked and knocked down by a group of white teenagers. He got up, shaken but unhurt, and went on into the waiting room. A layover had been planned at a college in Rock Hill, and while they were there Lewis was called back to Washington for a meeting. He left the riders, and then made arrangements to stop in Nashville and finish his final exams at the seminary before rejoining the ride in Montgomery. In the meantime, a bus on which the other group of riders was traveling was burned outside of Anniston, Alabama, and violence broke out in Birmingham. By the time Lewis got to Nashville, the SNCC leaders there were trying to get more volunteers to take up the ride in Birmingham, but there was a strong feeling in the older civil-rights groups that the rides shouldn't continue, and then CORE decided to withdraw its sponsorship of them. "The Nashville Christian Leadership Conference had the money to finance some more riders," Lewis recalls, "and we met with them until the early morning hours, begging for support. They said it was suicide, but we kept after them, and finally they agreed to put up the money for ten riders."

On the morning of May 17, the ten—including three girls—boarded a bus for Birmingham, with Lewis as their spokesman. On the outskirts of Birmingham, he remembers,

> *the bus was stopped by city police, and two guys in our group who were sitting closest to the front were arrested and taken away in a patrol car. When we got to the bus station, we weren't allowed to get off. Finally they led us into the waiting room, and after awhile Bull Connor and the mayor came, and we were taken into protective custody, as they called it. The Rev. Fred Shuttlesworth tried to get us released, and they arrested him too. We all went to jail—it was Wednesday afternoon by then—and we went on a hunger strike. In the early hours of Friday morning, Connor came in and offered to let us go if we'd promise not to continue the freedom ride, but we refused, so they picked us up and carried us to a limousine. There were seven of us by then—the two guys who had been taken off the bus were later released, and one girl had got away before we were arrested. Connor and his men started driving north, and he led us to believe he was going to take us all the way to Nashville, but when we got to Ardmore, right on the Tennessee line, at about 4 A.M., he put us out on the highway and told us to make it the best way we could.*

After walking a short distance in the darkness, they saw a little shack near a railroad crossing. Assuming—correctly, as it turned out—that Negroes lived there, they knocked on the door and finally roused an old man. He had heard about the trouble, and when he found out who they were he was reluctant to let them in, but finally he did. Lewis called Diane Nash and learned that ten more volunteers had been sent to take up the ride; he asked her to send a car to pick them up so they could go back, too. While they were waiting for the car, the old man went out for bread and milk and bologna, and they ate for the first time in three days.

The riders assembled later that day at Shuttlesworth's house in Birmingham, and then went to the station and waited for a bus to Montgomery. There was a large press contingent there, and when dark came a mob gathered outside the station. The riders waited inside all night, but no buses ran. Early the next morning they were able to board one, and at last they set out for the Alabama capital:

> *All along the way we saw state troopers, and small planes kept flying overhead. When we got into the station at Montgomery, there was nobody around, even though it was about ten o'clock in the morning. It was so quiet, kind of eerie. We stepped off the bus, and suddenly this angry, vicious mob started coming from all directions. They attacked the press, the girls, everybody. We finally got all the young ladies into a cab, but the driver was black, and he wouldn't move because two of the young ladies were white and it was against the law for a black cab to transport a white person. John Siegenthaler from the Justice Department was there, and he got between the mob and the girls somehow and got them into a church, but Siegenthaler was beaten. All of us were beaten, and left lying in the street. I don't know how long I was unconscious—I was hit over the head with a heavy object. All our suitcases and belongings were thrown into a pile and burned. It was pretty bad.*

Just how bad it was is difficult to comprehend. More than a score of people, most of them freedom riders, were injured, and violence spread through the city and continued sporadically for several days. The National Guard was called out, U.S. Marshals were sent in. The next day a mass meeting was held in Rev. Abernathy's church, and more mobs came. A smoke bomb was thrown into the church, and Governor John Patterson put the city under martial law and 1,200 people who were crammed into the church had to stay there through the night. Even after daylight came, it still took armed guardsmen to escort the people away from the church to safety. And in all that, press reports indicated that no instances of retaliation were discovered. The violence was all on the side of the white mobs.

Two days later, about forty freedom riders—Lewis among them—called a press conference to say they were going to Mississippi. They boarded two buses headed for Jackson, and rode with National Guard protection to the state line, where the Mississippi guard took over and escorted them the rest of the way. At the bus station all of the riders were arrested and taken to jail. They were run through a speedy trial, sentenced to sixty days, taken to the county prison farm—where some of them were beaten—and then to the Hinds County jail. At two o'clock one morning, they were taken out and moved to the state penitentiary at Parchman, 150 miles away. Lewis describes that experience:

> *It was a very frightening thing. I have never been more afraid in my life. They put the forty of us in a van, blacks and whites together—we had been segregated in our cells—and drove us to Parchman in the dark of night. The guards kept their guns drawn all the time, and they taunted us, told us we'd be killed when we got there. At Parchman we were forced to strip naked and wait for an hour and a half, without knowing what was going to happen to us. It was very dehumanizing. For the first time in my life, I was literally afraid, terrified. They herded us into cells, still naked, with guns pointed at our heads, and we waited another two hours. Then they forced us to take showers and to shave all beards and mustaches, and we were given a pair of green shorts and a t-shirt, and those were the only clothes we got for the thirty days we were there.*

After spending thirty-seven days under arrest, the riders were taken back to Jackson and released. John Lewis caught a train for Nashville:

> *My family never understood why I had become involved in all that. They had great fear of what it would all lead to, and they thought I was just going bad—getting in trouble with the law, going to jail and all that. I had lost any desire to be a preacher by then, and of course that troubled them too. So Nashville had become home for me. I did go back to Alabama to see my folks for a few days later that summer, but I needed contact with people who understood and supported me, and I couldn't get that kind of moral support at home. The Movement people became my family.*

That fall, John enrolled at Fisk University in Nashville to work for a degree in philosophy—he had been graduated in absentia from the American Baptist Theological Seminary, while he was on the freedom ride—and he was elected head of the Nashville Student Movement and made a member of SNCC's executive committee. For the next two years he continued to lead demonstrations for SNCC—in Nashville when school was going on, and in such places as Cairo, Illinois, and Charleston, Missouri, in the summers.

By the summer of 1963, discrimination was being challenged in dozens of locations across the South, and the philosophy of nonviolent resistance dominated most of those challenges. In Birmingham, Dr. King and hundreds of other Negroes went to jail, and police used high-pressure fire hoses and police dogs in a vain effort to repress a sustained protest against segregation; in Jackson, NAACP Field Secretary Medgar W. Evers was slain from ambush outside his home after leading a campaign to abolish segregation in the Mississippi capital; at the University of Alabama, the National Guard had to be federalized to make Governor George Wallace end his "stand in the schoolhouse door" and let two Negro students enroll. In the midst of these developments, SNCC held a meeting in Atlanta, and John Lewis became the new chairman. He left Fisk lacking only a few hours to complete his degree, and moved to Atlanta to begin his year in office.

As chairman of SNCC, Lewis joined with the leaders of the other major civil-rights organizations to plan the March on Washington. Looking back on it, that demonstration appears as the high-water mark of the nonviolent era. It brought the diverse elements of the civil-rights movement together for one massive show of unity, even as cracks were beginning to form beneath the surface. In his speech to the more than 200,000 people gathered at the Lincoln Memorial that August day, Lewis came off as the movement's angry young black man; his words were blunt and specific, in contrast to the more measured and less militant remarks of the "old guard"—Roy Wilkins, A. Philip Randolph, Whitney Young, and Martin Luther King. Even so, Lewis's remarks had been toned down the night before. He recalls:

> *I had written the speech in Atlanta, and I felt it was representative of the feelings of the people in SNCC and those we were working with. The day before the march, copies of all the speeches were distributed to the press, and that night, Bayard Rustin called me to a meeting to discuss it. I was told that Archbishop Patrick O'Boyle wouldn't give the invocation unless I changed my statement. In it, I had said we couldn't endorse President Kennedy's civil-rights bill—it was too little, too late—and I had said we couldn't be patient any longer, and I had said we would march through the South like Sherman did and burn Jim Crow to the ground—non-violently—and they were upset by all that. Mr. Randolph supported me on some of*

the points, but he said that for the sake of unity I should change the speech, so I did.

It was still a tough speech. Dr. King's famous "I have a dream" oration aspired to a future world of brotherhood; John Lewis's demanded "freedom now." But many of Lewis's compatriots in SNCC were disturbed and bitter that he had altered the speech, and many of the fractures which later spread through the Movement were already beginning in the student ranks. Paul Good, writing four years later in the *New York Times Magazine*, described the SNCC of mid-1963 as:

an organization already in flux, its original Southern element stirred by Northern recruits. Bohemianism was rubbing shoulders with old-time religion; nonviolence was alternately a creed and a tactic. Black Southern youth who saw salvation in the right to vote heard disillusioning Northern tales of ghettos that generations of black ballots could not vote away. Lewis was the embodiment of a deep paradox. Here was a young man of rural courtliness and moral high-mindedness, a square even, leading a group that generally disdained bourgeois manners and morals as just another American hangup.

For the next three years, while Lewis was serving as SNCC's chairman, the organization was represented just about everywhere that a civil-rights issue was raised—in the Alabama black belt and the Mississippi delta, in Maryland and Virginia, in Washington and New York and Atlanta. Lewis himself went from voter-registration campaigns, sit-ins, and demonstrations to speaking and fund-raising trips, from the jailhouse to the White House, and in all that he maintained the same curious mixture of manners and militancy that had marked his style since his first involvement in 1959. Later he remarked to a friend: "I learned early to pace myself. I felt we were involved in a lifetime struggle—hard, tedious, continuous. There were disappointments, but I had faith that continued pressure and pushing would pay off. I was still religious, but not in the traditional sense. You have to have a sense of hope and perseverance. You have to have a sense of hope to survive. I didn't give up, I didn't become bitter or become engulfed in hatred. That's just not a part of me."

After President Kennedy was killed, the civil-rights heat got hotter, and it was harder to find a focus in the movement. The Mississippi Freedom Summer followed; Chaney, Goodman, and Schwerner were murdered; Congress passed the

167

Civil Rights Act of 1964; the Johnson-Goldwater campaign prompted four civil-rights leaders—King, Wilkins, Young, and Randolph—to declare a moratorium on mass demonstrations until after the election. Lewis and James Farmer of CORE refused to join them. John didn't criticize the other organizations, but he felt that SNCC had its own role to play, and he kept at it in spite of complaints from the older organizations and from the radical wing of his own outfit. Lewis was on the SCLC board of directors, and he considered Martin Luther King his friend and his hero; he didn't hesitate to disagree with King, but he would not denounce him, and some of SNCC's left wing found it hard to accept such distinctions. There was Lewis, sticking to his belief in nonviolence, and to his support of white people in the movement, and to his friends in SCLC—his old schoolmates, James Bevel and Bernard Lafayette, were by then a part of King's team—and all of that clashed at times with the ideas and wishes of some other SNCC regulars, including James Forman, the executive secretary, and Stokely Carmichael, whose first trip South landed him in the pen at Parchman with the rest of the Freedom Riders.

Lewis won re-election to the chairmanship in 1964 and again in 1965. In 1964 he went to Africa on a trip arranged by Harry Belafonte, traveling with a group that included Mrs. Fannie Lou Hamer, Julian Bond, and Don Harris (his two closest friends in SNCC), Robert Moses, Jim Forman, and half a dozen others. Lewis and Harris traveled on alone to other parts of Africa after the group had stayed three weeks in Guinea as the guests of President Sekou Toure, and they were in Ethiopia when Johnson trounced Goldwater and Bobby Kennedy won a New York Senate seat.

Soon after he got back, the voter registration campaign was started in Selma, Alabama, and Lewis was among the first to be arrested there. Demonstrations went on there for more than two months, marked by some of the worst violence of the decade, and by the time the protracted demonstration was climaxed on the steps of the Alabama capitol in Montgomery after a march from Selma, at least three persons had been killed, scores injured (including Lewis, who was hospitalized after a beating by police), and hundreds jailed. And the speeches from the capitol steps that day sounded the same note of insistence and militant determination that had marked John Lewis's unedited statement at the March on Washington eighteen months before.

The Voting Rights Act of 1965 followed Selma. And Watts happened that summer, too—it was the first big explosion outside the South, and one of the growing number of signs that the civil-rights movement was undergoing rapid change. By the spring of 1966, Lewis had open opposition for re-election to the SNCC chairmanship:

I had been to Norway and elsewhere in Europe on a speaking tour, and when I got back just before our annual meeting in Nashville, Stokely Carmichael told me he would be a candidate. I believe he had run in 1965—he and several others—but I had won. I guess I was the representative of the Southern nonviolent philosophy—the main reason I was ever elected in the first place was that the Nashville movement was so well organized, and each year after that the dominant faction was the one I represented: pro-South, pro-nonviolence, pro-SCLC, pro-interracial.

We met for several days in May, at a retreat outside of Nashville. The night of the election there were about 200 people there, including several ex-SNCC people and others as observers. I was nominated for chairman, along with Stokely and one or two others. The vote was taken and I won by a large margin. Jim Forman had resigned as executive secretary, so Stokely was nominated for that post, but he declined. The election was closed. But then one of the ex-SNCC guys challenged the whole procedure, he challenged the election, and a big argument started. It got around to my relationship with Martin King, and my past contacts with the White House, and before it was over it got very low and nasty. Some people felt it was time for a change from nonviolence and integration to something else. King was considered an Uncle Tom, a sellout, white people were no longer wanted. It was a bitter night. Finally, the election was held over—many of the Southerners had left by then—and this time Stokely won by a big margin.

Earlier, Lewis had decided he would resign at the meeting and not run for re-election, but he changed his mind and stayed to fight it out. Part of his reason had to do with the North-South split in the ranks:

The Southern black students in SNCC had an altogether different outlook than the ones from the North. I don't know what it was exactly, but it always caused a tension, and it centered around nonviolence, and around how you react to people. The way it ended for me was a serious blow, a personal thing, and it affected me very much. I saw the end of the beginning. I saw the death of SNCC, of the movement. We had had a diverse group, reaching into all parts of the country, it had all been very new and hopeful.

As things turned out, Lewis's vision of the end was very nearly accurate. The following month, James Meredith started his one-man "march against fear" through Mississippi and was shot from ambush on the second day. Civil-rights leaders and supporters flocked to the state to take up his march, and Carmichael, with others, launched the "black power" rallying cry at every stop along the way. Lewis was there when the march reached Canton, and that night he spoke to the crowd. He talked about nonviolence, but it just wouldn't mix with the new mood: "I felt like an uninvited guest. It wasn't the same anymore, something was missing. I tried for a while to stay on in SNCC, but the position they were taking was inconsistent with my own convictions. Canton was the last scene for me. About a month later, I resigned from SNCC."

After that, Lewis went to work in New York for the Field Foundation, whose executive director, Leslie Dunbar, had formerly headed the Southern Regional Council in Atlanta. John didn't like New York; he missed the South, and after a little more than a year he went back to Atlanta to join the staff of SRC.

"You have to have a sense of hope to survive," he had said. Lewis's experiences could have made of him an underground guerrilla warrior, a true revolutionary. Instead, he emerged with as much faith, hope, and love as he had when it all started. Through something like double vision, he managed to see the good qualities in others—like John Kennedy and Lyndon Johnson—and his own imperfections, and that kind of vision makes only gentle revolutionaries.

Working in SRC's Community Organization Project with Al Ulmer, Lewis immersed himself again in the Southern struggle against discrimination and poverty. The headline figures had gone North, followed by the television cameras and the press corps. New civil-rights laws were on the books, and the issues had changed to Vietnam and the cities. It was quiet in Selma and Bogalusa and Americus. But for most blacks—and many poor whites—the necessities of food and shelter and employment and human dignity were as elusive as ever.

After John Kennedy was assassinated, Lewis gained a deeper respect and admiration for Bobby Kennedy than he had felt for him as attorney general: "I came to see him as the only political figure who could have bridged the gaps in this country and in the world, especially among the young and those who sought their freedom. There was something so basic, so good and passionate and understanding about him. He changed a lot after his brother was killed, he grew. The day he announced his candidacy for the Presidency in March 1968, I took leave from SRC and joined his campaign."

Lewis was with Kennedy in Indianapolis when Dr. King was assassinated. John was stunned by the news—his hero was dead—but he got another one that night: "Kennedy spoke at a rally after the news of Dr. King's death, and he did such a fine job, so sensitive, so fine. I saw his campaign then as an extension of the movement, as another step after the March on Washington, after Selma. Martin's death made it all the more important for me to work in Bobby's campaign, and I was able to transfer my loyalty to him."

From Indiana to Oregon to California, John worked as one of the RFK loyalists. The day before the California primary he witnessed

> *a tremendous outpouring of public support for him, and I knew the guy had something going for him. After the election the next day, I was in his room at the Ambassador Hotel. We were sure he had the victory sewed up, and everybody was in high spirits. Bobby laughed and said to me jokingly, "You let me down, John. The Mexican-Americans turned out better than the blacks." And then he asked some of us to wait there while he went down to make the victory speech. We were watching on TV when it happened.*

Bob Kennedy died, practically right before their eyes, and one more light went out for John Lewis. He wandered in a daze, down to the ballroom, then outside, then to the office Kennedy staffers had shared in a nearby hotel, then back to the Ambassador. Finally he stretched out on the floor somewhere and fell asleep, and then packed his bag and caught a plane for Atlanta. It was the end.

Or so it seemed. But the survival instinct prevailed, and hope returned. Later in the summer, Julian Bond led a challenge against the Georgia delegation to the Democratic Convention, and Lewis couldn't stay out of it. He went to Chicago with the Bond delegation, and cast his one-half vote for Teddy Kennedy. And when November came around, he couldn't bring himself to waste the first ballot he had ever cast in a Presidential election. He considered the choices pragmatically, and voted for Hubert Humphrey.

Lewis is married now. He and his wife, Lillian, live in Atlanta, and he still works for the Southern Regional Council. He goes back to Troy more often than he once did: "My family remains active in the church—my father is a deacon—and they more or less think I've lost my way, but I think they're coming to understand better what I've tried to say and do. We're closer now than in a long time. I've tried consciously not to separate myself from my family. I have a deep love for them, for the outdoors, for what I consider home."

Home is the South. Lewis says:

> *I think in the South we've all been the victims of violence and brutality, both those who have suffered it and those who have practiced it. We've all lived in it. There's a degree of humanity about Southerners that's perhaps different from people elsewhere. There's an element of human understanding, of compassion, and we have that to build on simply because of what we've been through. It can become real. We can be more loving, more forgiving; we can more readily understand. We're going through a transitional period now, but I don't think it will be with us long. I have abiding faith that something good and positive will emerge. We can't continue on this level. All the violence, the wars, the riots, the assassinations, it's all too much. It will have to force the best out of us, the true good. I believe it.*

There is no doubt that he does. John Lewis dreams things that never were, and says why not.

John Lewis was elected in 1986 to represent Atlanta in the U.S. Congress, and has since been re-elected five times.

REBECCA WELLS

HAIR OF THE DOG
{Siddalee, 1965}

from *Little Altars Everywhere*

IT'S SATURDAY morning and we are all riding over to the Hotsy-Totsy Room with Mama and Caro, one of Mama's best buddies. We have to get Mama's high-heel from under the *porte cachère* where she forgot it the night before.

Little Shep, Lulu, Baylor, and I are packed into the back seat of the T-Bird like sardines, and Mama and Caro have the air conditioner cranked up full-blast. Caro spent the night with us at Pecan Grove, even though Mama originally started out the night with Daddy, who ended up not coming home at all. When Mama and Caro woke the whole house up coming in, I took one of Mama's Nytols that I had stashed in my nightstand and went back to sleep. But Lulu must have stayed up all night. When I got up, she looked all dazed and she had another picked-at red spot on her head.

I said, Jesus, Lulu, have you been at it again? I don't see how anybody can actually eat their own hair.

She said, Siddy, I *try* not to. Really.

I know, I said, and rubbed a dab of Vaseline on the spot. Now don't pick at it anymore today, you hear me?

In the front seat of the car, Caro and Mama are wearing sunglasses, even though it's overcast outside. I put on my sunglasses too. We just pull up in front of the Hotsy-Totsy Room, and without the car hardly coming to a stop, Caro opens the door and scoops up Mama's ice blue sling-back pump, and we drive off.

The Hotsy-Totsy Room is the only cocktail dance lounge of its kind in Thornton and it is very popular because of the Ya-Yas—Mama's gang of girlfriends—and their crowd. It's a stucco building with sparkles built into it. Seashells are set in the concrete driveway, and at night, twinkly lights shine in the bushes. Every time Mama and Daddy walk in there, the band stops whatever they're doing and plays "Moon River," Mama and Daddy's favorite song.

After we pick up the high-heel, Mama pulls out onto the service road and says, Sidda, reach into that ice chest and get Caro and me those cold rags, will you?

I hand them the rags and they each put one on their forehead.

What's wrong with yall's heads, Mama? Little Shep asks.

We don't know, Mama says.

We both caught one of those little bugs that's going around, Caro explains. And they both give a little laugh.

Mama turns to Caro and says, I don't know about you, girl, but I'm sick as a dog.

Make that two dogs, Caro mumbles. Drive a little smoother, will you?

Well, I've got those damn little floaties in front of my eyes, Mama says. They don't make for the best driving I've ever done in my life.

Well, says Caro, we have got to stay on the move. I cannot bear the thought of seeing either one of those men we married until I feel a little more up to snuff.

Plus, Mama says, pressing her finger to her right temple, I don't want the party to end. It's hell this morning, but it was heaven last night. I haven't danced like that since high school.

You finally had some decent dance partners again, Vivi—that's why.

Mama says, Little pitchers have big ears.

I stare out the window and act like I'm not listening to every word that comes out of their mouths.

Hell, Caro says, you know damn well Shep has never been a dancer. The man might be able to grow cotton, but he's a slew-footed clod on the dance floor.

Mama giggles and says, He tries.

That's about the extent of it, Caro says, he *tries*.

Well, it didn't slow me down any, Mama brags.

That's an understatement, Caro laughs. We were magnificent! We danced with every man in the place at least twice.

Yeah, Mama says, until we wore them out or teed off their wives and had to start dancing with each other. Hell, Chick's the only male who can keep up with us. I knew I should've married him instead of letting Teensy have him.

He was too short for you in high school, Vivi, and he's too short for you now, Caro says.

Well, he still could grow, Mama says and laughs.

Anyway, it was glorious, Caro says. Just like the old days. And, of course, those diet pills didn't hurt.

Not one bit, Mama says. Then she turns around and looks at the four of us. How yall doing, spooks? Yall hungry?

Yes ma'am, we all say.

Hold on then, Mama says, We'll get something in your pitiful stomachs before you know it.

We didn't eat any breakfast or anything. Mama didn't even try to fix my hair like she does every morning. My hair is almost down to my waist, and if it isn't done in a certain way it just drives Mama to the insane asylum. She says with all my hair I could easily look like poor white trash or a Pentecostal if I'm not careful. This morning, though, she completely forgets about my hair, and I'm glad, because the way she usually whips it around feels like she really is trying to jerk me bald-headed. She always says, That's the price you have to pay for beauty, Siddalee.

The thing is, Caro says, Shep gets so burned up when the Ya-Yas get together. It makes me want to kill him, the way he talked to you last night. Saying: "You have never known how to act in public, Vivi." Caro says this in a voice like Daddy's.

Well, Mama says, Shep was raised different than we were.

That's no excuse for him to drive off and spend the night at the goddamn duck camp, Caro says. If Chick hadn't driven us home, then I don't know what we would've done. It's not like Thornton is New York City when it comes to taxicabs at four A.M.

Then she just snorts like she does not have the energy to go any further.

Don't you have a pillow anywhere in this car? she asks Mama. Mama lets Caro boss her around and criticize her like nobody else ever can.

Caro holds her wet rag in front of the air-conditioner vent, then lays it over her whole face and leans back against the door.

Mama drives real slow and careful—until she comes to an intersection and then she speeds across real fast, stepping on the gas like she's afraid someone will slam into her. Then she slows down again and crawls the car along the street until she comes to the next intersection. We stop and fill up the car at Roland's Texaco and then Mama drives us in fits and starts over to Ship-Shape Donuts.

She leaves the car running, hands me ten dollars, and says, Go get whatever yall want. Get us two huge coffees, black.

They stay in the car and we run in and get a dozen donuts and some cinnamon rolls and Lulu gets four of her rum balls. She hordes those rum balls and eats them on the sly. We all get Cokes too, even though Daddy says that having a cold drink before twelve noon is "a whore's breakfast."

Back in the car, those donuts are so soft and squashy and sweet, all warm out of the oven, and we sit in the back seat of the T-Bird and just eat and eat. Ooh, all that sugar and those Cokes on crushed ice just go down so good.

Mama looks in the rear-view mirror and says, Lulu, put that donut back in the bag right this instant.

Lulu says, Oh Mama, why?

Mama says, Just do what I say. Trust me, you will live to regret that donut if you eat it. I am only trying to save you from growing up to be a lard-ass like the women on your daddy's side of the family.

Do you think a cigarette will kill me? she asks Caro.

I would not touch a ciggie with a ten-foot pole, Caro says. Not until I swallow a hair of the dog that bit me.

Mama sighs, Thank God I have the Ya-Yas to tell me what to do.

Where in the hell are we going next? Caro asks.

Mama says, Who cares? Let's bomb over to Chick and Teensy's and see if they're up yet. I hope they feel just as bad as we do.

Fine, Caro says, just fine. And she settles back with the cold air blowing on her.

Mama pulls the car out onto the almost empty street. Where is everybody? It feels like we're in a sort of Twilight Zone town.

Little Shep pulls out his Etch-a-Sketch and Lulu says, Let me play!

Little Shep says, Shut up, Porky.

She starts to cry and I say, Yall cut that out. Mama doesn't feel good.

Lulu sits there sucking on a strand of her hair and I give her a look like: You remember what I told you, Baldy.

I pull *Nancy Drew and the Mystery of Lilac Inn* out of my purse and try to forget where I am. The car is so crowded there isn't even enough room for us to hardly sit, let alone stash any of our stuff. So we have to squinch in together and it is horrible being that crammed in. Mama and Daddy had a big fight over Mama getting the T-Bird because it's only built to seat four. But Mama says if she's going to haul us all over the place, she's going to do it in the car of her choice. When the six of us have to go somewhere together as a whole family, Daddy just follows behind in his truck.

After four or five blocks, Mama says, I simply *cannot* drive another inch. Caro, you have *got* to take over, the floaties are killing me.

Caro groans, You think I've got it any better? When are these kids going to start being good for something? Let one of them drive.

We should be so lucky, Mama says, and starts to slide toward the passenger seat. They climb over each other, because neither one of them is about to step outside into the heat. Caro gets in the driver's seat and Mama props her foot up on the dash and complains: If we didn't have kids we could have cars with tinted windows. We're martyrs, that's what we are: martyrs to the cause.

Caro laughs. She says, Blaine is probably still sound asleep and I bet the boys are tearing my house to shreds. Let them. I'm sick of that rat-trap anyway.

And they both laugh and turn on the radio to some Easy Listening. The Ya-Yas love Easy Listening whenever they catch one of their bugs.

At Teensy and Chick's we pull into the driveway and pile out of the car. Mama raps on the kitchen door like shave-and-a-haircut, two bits! She says, They damn well better have a pitcher of Bloody Marys ready.

Ruffin, who is my age, answers the door. He still has on his cowboy pajamas.

Mama says, Hi, Ruff, where're your Mama and Daddy?

Ruffin crosses his arms and says, They're still asleep. Yall better not wake them up or they'll kill you.

Caro says, Good boy! Then she and Mama push past him into the kitchen. We trail in behind them.

I say, Hi, Ruffin.

He says, Yall better get out of here, I mean it. Yall better not make any noise.

All over the kitchen counters there are those tiny cereal boxes you can eat right out of and you can smell burnt toast in the air.

Ruffin says, Really, Vivi, if you wake them up they're gonna be really mad. They don't feel good.

Well honey, Mama says, *we don't either,* and we want some company. Now take all the kids and yall go play in traffic.

Ruffin stands there looking stupid and hurt.

Mama gives him a hug and says, Ruff dahling, I'm just *kidding!* Now yall go watch some TV.

Ruffin mumbles, Our antenna is broken.

Mama ignores him, and says to Caro, Plan 27-B (which is their code for: move on, no matter what). The two of them head back to Teensy and Chick's bedroom. The door is shut and you can hear their big window air conditioner blasting away inside.

Ruffin gives one last warning: I mean it, they're not going to like this.

But Mama and Caro burst into Chick and Teensy's room and just jump in the bed with them, and yell: Get up! Yall think yall can sleep all day while we're awake suffering?! Get up!

We stand at the door and watch. Teensy's nightclub dress is on the chair next to the bed, and she has on this poofy peignoir. Teensy props herself up in bed and stares at Mama and Caro like they are Ubangis. It looks like there are pieces of red thread stuck to her eyeballs.

You damn fools! she says. Get out of here. Yall think because I'm the only Ya-Ya with a fun husband you can come in here and wake me up like this?

Chick just rolls over without opening his eyes. He kind of waves his hand like he's swatting flies. Chick is real little and wiry and cute, kind of like a horse jockey. He is sort of an honorary male Ya-Ya. When his hand reaches out, you can see his silk pajama sleeve. I never realized grown men actually slept in pajamas except in movies. Daddy always sleeps in his boxer shorts.

Come on Teensy! Mama says. Come on Chick! Don't yall want to get up and play? We drove all the way over here just to commiserate.

The hell yall did, Teensy growls, and turns her pillow over to the cool side. Yall came over here because you're scared to death to face Blaine and Shep. I can't *believe* some of the stunts yall pulled last night. Yall were out of control, even for Ya-Yas.

We didn't do anything you wouldn't have done if you hadn't married Chick, Mama says.

Teensy says, Yall are terrible, now get out of here. Go find somebody else to torture.

Mama and Caro just keep lying on the bed like they think she is kidding.

I'm serious, Teensy yells. Yall go on. Chick and I are going to sleep till three, then get up and have eggs Benedict. Hit the road.

Party-poopers! Caro says.

What a bunch of spooks, Mama says. Then Mama and Caro both climb out of the bed and start to lead us out to the car, but not without checking the liquor cabinets first.

Where is your mama's vodka? Caro asks Ruffin.

I don't know, Ruffin says, she hides it.

Oh well, Mama says, and gives Ruffin a kiss on the forehead. Then she opens the kitchen door and we all walk out again into the hot gray day and climb into the hot stuffy car.

Mama and Caro look at each other and Caro says, Those SOBs. I was *counting* on them for a Bloody.

Mama says, Well, we can have one of the beers out of the cooler.

I will die before I drink any of that alligator piss, Caro says. I need a real drink.

Mama looks at Caro and says, *Abra!*

Caro winks at her and says, *Cadabra!*

Then Caro guns the car in the direction of Davis Street, which means the Abracadabra Liquor store.

Usually we go to the Abracadabra at night when Mama and Daddy run out of something or need to stock up. They go inside and leave us in the back of Daddy's pickup. It's always dark all around us, with the only light coming from the blazing fluorescent lights inside the store and the sign that hangs out front.

The Abracadabra sign is huge pastel-colored neon about the size of a Brahma bull. You just can't help but be in awe of it. At the top of the sign is an angel with a skull for a face. Its neon wings pulsate so fast that it looks like the angel is panicked, like it's trying to get away from something. When the bottom of the angel flicks back and forth, it looks like a serpent tail stabbing the night air. Underneath the angel, the name "Abracadabra" is spelled out with the kind of little white bulbs that movie stars have on their dressers. Below that, the words "Liquor, Party Foods, Ice, and Gifts" pulse in green, pink, yellow, and blue. Just the letters in those words are scary to look at, like they have a mysterious power that nothing can control. That panicked angel lights up the four of us in the back of Daddy's truck and makes us easy targets for all those things that hide in the dark. If there are stars in the sky, you can't even see them because that sign blinds your eyes to anything else.

The place isn't nearly so spooky during the day. We pull up to the drive-up window and Mama and Caro order a fifth of Smirnoff and a bunch of V-8 juice from a guy with a transistor radio playing the colored music station. Daddy never lets us listen to that station. The Ya-Yas love it though.

Mama says, Just put that on Shep Walker's account, dahling.

Then she turns around to us and says, Yall want anything?

Yeah, I say, some Fritos.

What did you say? Mama asks me.

I correct myself: *Yes ma'am,* we would love some Fritos. Thank you for asking.

That's better, Mama says. Throw in a couple bags of Frito-Lays, would you, Tony?

The man says, We ain't got no Fritos, just pigskins.

Okay then, pigskins, Mama tells him and he flips three bags of pigskins into the back seat. I am not about to touch them. Eating the skin of dead pigs fried in their own bacon grease is something I will not do, even if I'm starving to death on a desert island.

Of course, Lulu snorks them right down and Little Shep says, Hey Porky, why don't you inhale them through your snout?!

It's not that Lulu is really all that fat. She just has a round little face and cheeks that make her look chubbier than she is. Still, it's a habit for everyone to pick on her for being a little fatty. You can upset her with it every time, so we tease her just because it's so much fun.

Mama and Caro mix up some drinks in Dixie cups, then we head out again. Mama lights up a cigarette and things are looking better. It's cool in the car and the cigarette smoke smells familiar.

Then, out of the blue, Caro pulls over to the side of the road and slams on the brakes, opens the door, leans her head out, and throws up on the street. Son of a bitch, she says. Son of a goddamn bitch!

Mama says, You poor baby. You alright?

Oh I'm fine. Never been better. It's your damn cigarette. I told you, I cannot handle smoke until I've had the chance to get a drink down.

I'm so sorry, babydoll, Mama says, and she takes her wet cloth and dabs Caro's face with it.

You want a Lifesaver to take the taste out? Should I take you home?

God no, Caro says. You just drive. I'll be fine, once I get down a drink or two. And don't you dare light up another ciggie or I will strangle you with my bare hands.

So Mama gets behind the wheel and she says, I just hope the floaties don't cause me to run this damn T-Bird into the ditch. She sits there for a minute idling the motor, sipping her Bloody Mary. Then she says—like it's the most original idea she's ever had and she should get an award for it: I've got it! We'll drive out to Lucille's! She's always ready for a party!

Caro is mixing another drink, mumbling, These Dixie cups are so damn tiny.

Well Caro, Mama asks, what do you think?

Inspired, Vivi dahling, simply inspired. Drive on.

You can tell they're both starting to feel a little better as we drive down the tree-lined state highway to Natchitoches. Miss Lucille lives alone up on Cane River in this huge antebellum house. She divorced her husband and took him for every cent he had. She's older than the Ya-Yas and they all worship her. She's sort of their living idol. Miss Lucille was once a very famous horsewoman until she was thrown by her favorite horse. And she just quit riding after that. She told everyone it wasn't that she was hurt or anything, it was just the way that horse had betrayed her.

Sometimes she just shows up in Thornton in her chocolate brown Cadillac to do some shopping, and a whole party will start up just because she is in town. Mama and the Ya-Yas have known her for years—ever since they were in New Orleans one weekend on a shopping trip and they met her one night at the Carousel Room in the Monteleone Hotel. They just fell in love with her, and all of them ended up riding the train back together, and they have been friends ever since.

Miss Lucille's house is a huge place at the end of this long drive of oak trees with trailing Spanish moss all over them. The house has eight big white columns across the front and this deep veranda upstairs and down. It's the kind of gracious old home that the Ya-Yas adore visiting, but you couldn't *give* them a place like that because there isn't any central air-conditioning or a dishwasher.

We pull up the long drive, with Mama blowing the horn like she always does. All of us have our eyes glued to the windows to catch a glimpse of Miss Lucille naked. Miss Lucille is an artist now and she always works on her sculptures while she's buck naked. We can barely see her throw on her kimono and tie the sash before the T-Bird comes to a stop in her circular drive.

She runs out shouting at the top of her lungs. Vivi! Caro! *Petits monstres!* Hey!

Miss Lucille always shouts. It isn't that she is hard-of-hearing, she just loves to talk loud, Mama says. Around her you have to shout back, or there just isn't any conversation. Sometimes the way she yells, you don't know whether she is really really happy to see you, or whether she is mad at you for invading her privacy.

Lucille, dahling! Mama shouts back, although you can see her wince like it's killing her head.

They all hug each other like it's been fifty years since they've gotten together.

Miss Lucille uses a long cigarette holder and smokes like Marlene Dietrich. Every time you watch her take a puff, you think you're in Europe. Her hair is gray everywhere, except in front where it's bright red. And she has these large hands that look like a pretty man's. Mama and the Ya-Yas love playing *bourrée* with her because she's such a superior cheater. They claim they learned everything they know about cheating from her.

She says, Well, what are we drinking? G&Ts?

We follow her through the house and she stops to put an Edith Piaf record on the stereo. Then we go into the big kitchen, where she mixes up a huge pitcher of gin and tonic like it is lemonade. Miss Lucille has five golden retrievers that lounge around inside that house, and they yelp and growl when we (accidentally) step on their tails. Those dogs just go with Miss Lucille's house, like they're mink coats or something draped across the furniture.

Baylor stares around the house, peeking in every room we pass, like he always does. He says, I'm gonna have me a house just like this when I grow up.

Miss Lucille hands Mama and Caro their G&Ts, and then says to Bay, Well, Handsome, are you still going to come live with me as soon as you turn eighteen?

When she winks at him, he goes over and holds onto Mama's leg. But Mama says, Bay, honey, don't hang all over me, please. Not today.

Lulu says, Miss Lucille, can I go upstairs and take a nap? She does this every single time we come here. She has a thing about those bedrooms.

Miss Lucille has fans set up everywhere you turn, and it makes you almost forget how hot and sticky it is without air-conditioning.

Caro says, You *must* show us what you've been working on, 'Cille.

Love to, Miss Lucille says, absolutely love to.

They always ask to see her sculptures. But whenever I ask Mama about Miss Lucille, Mama says, Honey, Lucille is more an artist in her *mind* than anything else. (Mama also says you're not a real artist unless you live in New York City.)

Miss Lucille takes us on a tour of her sculptures, which are all over the house and out on the veranda. Every single one she points to, she says, Of course it's *unfinished*. You can see that for yourself.

One particular sculpture scares me to death. Miss Lucille calls it "The Sleeping Bitch." It has been at her house for as long as I can remember. It is a woman taking a nap. Her whole body looks relaxed except for her face—which looks like it's witnessing something so horrible her eyes could burn up. Her mouth looks like she's trying to scream, but can't get any sound out. It always reminds me of a dream I have where I'm grunting and sweating, but I can't squeeze out one single sound. Every time I see that sculpture there is something ever so slightly different about it, like Miss Lucille works on it for about five minutes a month.

After we view the art, the ladies settle in the canvas butterfly chairs out on the veranda, and Little Shep and me go out in the yard to play. Over beyond the cedars are millions of crepe myrtle trees and during the summer they're all rose-colored. I like the way all that rose color looks against those black cedars, and sometimes I kind of relax my eyes so that it all blends together. Little Shep and me have this game we play, where his name is Barry and mine is Jennifer. Whenever we use those names, we feel great. It doesn't matter what we're doing, as long as we do it as Barry and Jennifer. We're playing "Barry and Jennifer in the Civil War" behind the crepe myrtles, and it is so hot, you just know the Yankees are coming. Then, out of nowhere, we get one of those afternoon rains that cools things off and makes the air smell fresh.

We stand out there and let ourselves get soaking wet. The sun is starting to peek out from behind that scum of gray sky, and light trickles down through the cedars. The rain stops as quick as it comes, and we're standing in a real clean spot and we both know it.

Little Shep says in a fake accent, Jennifer, shall we go back to the big house?

I say, Oh yes, Barry, let's.

And we hold each other's hands, like we never do when we're our real selves. My hair is hanging down heavy on my shoulders and when the water drips, it tickles and feels good on my skin.

We walk back to the veranda and Mama eyes me like she's never seen me before, like she's studying me. I pull my halter-top down where it's slid up a little. I don't know why she is looking at me like that. I haven't done anything.

Without taking her eyes off me, she announces, Siddalee, you are too grown-up to have all that hair hanging down to your butt!

Then she grinds out her cigarette in a crystal ashtray that is full of butts and says to Caro, Why don't you give Sidda one of your haircuts? It's something that's long overdue.

Caro is famous for cutting hair, not like a real beautician but just when she feels like it. She cut her own hair in all these different angles and she looks sort of like a skinny Ingrid Bergman. She gets up and lifts my hair off my neck and twists it softly in her hand. I have always been a sucker for anyone who wants to touch my head, as long as they're not pulling at it the way Mama does.

It's so thick, Caro says. This is just too much hair. Don't you get tired of the weight of it, Sidda?

I have never gotten tired from my hair before, but I say, Yes ma'am, I do. I just get exhausted sometimes.

I adore having them all look at my hair. They all get into the act. Miss Lucille runs and gets some yellow-handled kitchen scissors and a brush and hand mirror. They sit me on a stool on the veranda and Caro starts cutting. I close my eyes and just listen to the scissors and the dripping of the rain off the magnolia leaves and the sound of Mama's cigarette lighter when she snaps it open. It's so quiet, you can even hear the tiny *whiff* sounds my hair makes when it hits the brick veranda floor. I sit there and feel all their eyes focused just on me. Caro lifts my hair and snips and touches my head. And I kind of float away from the veranda into the trees.

When I open my eyes, fifteen inches of my hair is on the brick floor.

Caro hands me the mirror and says, *Voila!*

When I look at myself, I resemble the pictures of Heidi's friend Peter. I don't even look like a girl. My chest closes up. I feel all naked. I feel like they've cut off my legs or my arms, not just my hair.

You are magnificent! Mama says, and jumps up from her chair to examine me. She ruffles her hands through my hair and I can feel her fingernails against my scalp. My head is so bare, it's like she could push her fingernails down into my skull if she wanted and leave permanent dents. Her cigarette smoke curls around me and I can smell the lime in her drink.

You have never looked better! she pronounces. My God, you are gorgeous! Caro, you are an artist.

Then she says, Little Shep, go find a broom and trash can and sweep up this mess! And she gestures to my cut-off hair like it's dog poop under our feet.

Caro winks at me and says, Sidda, get ready dahling, the boys are gonna really come sniffing around now.

Miss Lucille doesn't say anything. She just stares at me like she wants to ask a question.

Do you like it, Miss Lucille? I ask her.

What does it matter what I think? she says. What does it matter what anybody thinks about anything?

I look down at my reddish-brown hair lying on the bricks. The bricks and my hair are about the same color. I can feel tiny bits of hair sticking to my skin, like they don't want to let go of my body. I get up and stand in front of the fan and lift up the back of my shirt to try and let the hair blow off me. My hair has been long since I was a real little girl, and without it I feel cockeyed and dizzy. Like losing the weight of my hair has thrown me off-balance. I was used to how I had looked for so long and how my hair felt when I reached up to roll it between my fingers. When I was alone, I used to hold a clump of my hair and just smell it. And that would make me feel good because it was my smell and it made me feel more *there.*

I stand by the fan and try to get used to the new me. *Why did I lie and say I was tired of my hair? When really, it was the main thing about me that I loved?* I ruin everything, I think. I ruin it all. I feel like crying, but I can't. I brought this all on myself.

Baylor, who was sitting on the steps watching the whole thing, gets up and does something that surprises me. He bends down and picks up a lock of my hair and puts it in his pocket. He looks at it and smells it and puts it in his pocket.

Mama watches him and says, My youngest has always been a little strange.

Miss Lucille says, I see nothing strange about him whatsoever. And she walks into her house and comes back out with an envelope that she hands to Baylor. Here, she says. You can keep it in this.

Thank you, Miss Lucille, he says very seriously.

Then he reaches into his pocket, takes out my hair, and places it in the gray envelope that has "Lucille Romaine, Cane River, Natchitoches, Louisiana" embossed on it.

I say, Bay, why are you doing that?

He mumbles, It's not really for me. It's for someone else.

And I say to my little brother, Where do you *come* from?

The sun is setting by then. Miss Lucille lights some mosquito torches and the smell drifts through the air, covering up all the other smells. She turns on the veranda lamps and hands Mama and Caro some Six-Twelve to rub on.

Miss Lucille says, Here, Vivi, let me rub some on your back. That's where those damn things always get me, right under my bra.

And she sticks her hand under Mama's shirt and smears on some insect repellent, and then they get out the cards so they can really start having a party.

Not too long afterward, Lulu comes down the stairs from her nap. I'm hungry, she says. I'm starving. When she sees me, she seems confused, like she isn't completely sure who I am.

There is never anything to eat at Miss Lucille's, so we just go into her kitchen and scrounge around till we find some crackers and anchovy paste and a little leftover tonic. The whole time Little Shep and Baylor and Lulu keep staring at my hair.

Finally Little Shep says, Sidda, you look like a mop.

Baylor says, Siddy, can we put your hair back on?

It gets dark and it looks like nobody is going anywhere. So the four of us watch TV for a long time in Miss Lucille's den. Finally we get tired and turn it off and fall asleep on the couch and chairs.

I don't know how long we doze, but I'm the first one to smell it. I yell, Yall get up! Something's burning!

We all run out to the veranda and we find the ladies screaming and screaming, going crazy everywhere because the trash can filled with my hair is on fire. Mama is standing there with an empty ashtray in her hand.

Caro says, You fool! You should never have emptied that! I hadn't stubbed my ciggie out yet.

Well, Mama says, I was getting sick of looking at all those damn dead butts.

The three of them just stand there staring at the blazing trash can, amazed—like it is more than they can ever cope with.

I can taste anchovy in my mouth, and I wish I could brush my teeth. The smell of my hair on fire is awful. I did not know that something cut off of me could really smell that bad.

Little Shep runs into the kitchen and comes back with a decanter full of water. He dumps it into the can and the fire goes out. Just like that.

Miss Lucille says, Oh it is so good to have a man around the house! Now let's all just take a couple of Bufferin, spray a little perfume out here, and everything will be fine.

We spend the night at Miss Lucille's without even calling Daddy. I wake up real early the next morning before anybody else opens their eyes. My hands shoot straight up to my head where my hair used to be. *I miss it. I want it back.* I don't look in any of the mirrors. I rub my hands across my scalp. My hair feels more like a hat than hair. Like it is a bird's head, not my own.

I walk out into the yard and there is still dew on the grass, although you can tell the day will be another scorcher. I go out behind the cedars and over by the crepe myrtles. I stand there for a minute, feeling far away from everything because it's still so early. Then I lie down on the grass. It's cool and damp, and it itches and feels good at the same time. I can see the sky above me just coming to light, and the fringes of the cedar and all the pink of the crepe myrtles. There aren't any bugs or mosquitoes, nothing to bite me. I lie on my back in the grass for a long time and then I turn over and lie on my stomach. My heart starts pounding, my breath gets real tight, and I get all afraid.

But I can feel the ground underneath me. And I tell myself: The earth is holding me up. I am lighter than I was before. My hair is like grass planted on the top of my head. If I can just wait long enough, maybe it will grow back in some other season.

EXCHANGE OF THE IDEA

BY

PETER SÍS

LEE SMITH

Terrain of the Heart

ALTHOUGH I don't usually write autobiographical fiction, my main character in a recent short story sounded suspiciously like the girl I used to be: "More than anything else in the world, I wanted to be a writer. I didn't want to learn to write, of course. I just wanted to be a writer, and I often pictured myself poised at the foggy edge of a cliff someplace in the south of France, wearing a cape, drawing furiously on a long cigarette, hollow-cheeked and haunted. I had been romantically dedicated to the grand idea of 'being a writer' ever since I could remember."

I started telling stories as soon as I could talk—true stories, and made-up stories, too. My father was fond of saying that I would climb a tree to tell a lie rather than stand on the ground to tell the truth. In fact, in the mountains of southwestern Virginia where I grew up, a lie was often called a story, and well do I remember being shaken until my teeth rattled with the stern admonition, "Don't you tell me no story, now!"

But I couldn't help it. I was already hooked on stories, and as soon as I could write, I started writing them down.

I wrote my first book on my mother's stationery when I was nine. It featured as main characters my two favorite people at that time: Adlai Stevenson and Jane Russell. The plot was that they went west together in a covered wagon, and once there they became—inexplicably—Mormons. Even at that age, I was fixed upon glamour and flight, two themes I returned to again and again as I wrote my way through high school, fueled by my voracious reading. My book choices proceeded alphabetically: the *B*'s for instance included Hamilton Basso, the Brontes, . . . At St. Catherine's School in Richmond, during my last two years of high school, I was gently but firmly guided toward the classics, but my own fiction remained relentlessly sensational.

At Hollins College, I wrote about stewardesses living in Hawaii, about evil twins, executives, alternative universes. I ignored my teachers' instructions to write what you know. I didn't know what they meant. I didn't know what I knew. I certainly didn't intend to write anything about Grundy, Virginia.

But then Louis Rubin, my teacher, had us read the stories of Eudora Welty, and a light went on in my head. I abandoned my stewardesses, setting my feet on more familiar ground, telling simpler stories about childhood; though I was never able, somehow, to set the stories in those mountains I came from.

This never happened until I encountered James Still—all by myself, perusing the *S*'s in the Hollins College library.

Here I found the beautiful and heartbreaking novel *River of Earth*, a kind of Appalachian *Grapes of Wrath* chronicling the Baldridge family's desperate struggle to survive when the mines close and the crops fail, familiar occurrences in Appalachian life. Theirs is a constant odyssey, always looking for something better someplace else—a better job, a better place to live, a promised land. As the mother says, "Forever moving, yon and back, setting down nowhere for good and all, searching for God knows what. . . . Where are we expecting to draw up to?"

At the end of the novel, I was astonished to read that the family was heading for—of all places!—"Grundy."

"I was born to dig coal," Father said. "Somewhere they's a mine working. I been hearing of a new mine farther than the head of Kentucky River, on yon side Pound Gap. Grundy, its name is. . . ."

I read this passage over and over. I simply could not believe that Grundy was in a novel! In print! Published! Then I finished reading *River of Earth* and burst into tears. Never had I been so moved by a book. In fact, it didn't seem like a book at all. *River of Earth* was as real to me as the chair I sat on, as the hollers I'd grown up among.

Suddenly, lots of the things of my life occurred to me for the first time as stories: my mother and my aunts sitting on the porch talking endlessly about whether one of them had colitis or not; Hardware Breeding, who married his wife, Beulah, four times; how my uncle Curt taught my daddy to drink good liquor; how I got saved at the tent revival; John Hardin's hanging in the court-house square; how Petey Chaney rode the flood. . . .

I started to write these stories down. Twenty-five years later, I'm still at it. And it's a funny thing: Though I have spent most of my working life in univer-sities, though I live in Chapel Hill and eat pasta and drive a Toyota, the stories which present themselves to me as worth the telling are most often those some-how connected to that place and those people. The mountains which used to imprison me have become my chosen stalking ground.

This is the place where James Still lives yet, in an old log house on a little eastern Kentucky farm between Wolfpen Creek and Deadmare Branch. Still was born in Alabama in 1906; went to Lincoln Memorial University in Cumberland Gap, Tennessee, and then to Vanderbilt; and came to Knott County, Kentucky, in 1932 to "keep school" at the forks of Troublesome Creek.

After six years, as he likes to tell it, he "retired" and turned to reading and writing full time. As one of his neighbors said, "He's left a good job and come over in here and sot down."

Last summer he told me he had read an average of three hours a day, every day, for over fifty years. His poetry and fiction have been widely published and praised; his *Wolfpen Notebooks* came out in 1991 from the University Press of Kentucky.

In the preface to that fine collection of sayings and notes he has made over all these years, Still says:

> *Appalachia is that somewhat mythical region with no known borders. If such an area exists in terms of geography, such a domain as has shaped the lives and endeavors of men and women from pioneer days to the present and given them an independence and an outlook and a vision such as is often attributed to them, I trust to be understood for imagining the heart of it to be in the hills of Eastern Kentucky where I have lived and feel at home and where I have exercised as much freedom and peace as the world allows.*

This is an enviable life, to live in the terrain of one's heart. Most writers don't—can't—do this. Most of us are always searching, through our work and in our lives: for meaning, for love, for home.

Writing is about these things. And as writers, we cannot choose our truest material. But sometimes we are lucky enough to find it.

SANDRA
KITT

It's All in Our Heads

SOMETHING extraordinary and magical happened to me when I was about six or seven years old. I discovered that behind my eyelids there was a movie screen. And the projector—I guess today we would call it the VCR—was between my eyes and glued onto my brain. I then found out that both were activated when I sat down and read a book. The words on the pages of books formed sentences that told stories, and the stories made pictures in my head. Not only could I read what was going on . . . I could see the action taking place on that movie screen of my mind. The children in the stories I read as a child came alive. I would never meet them, of course, but I grew to love many of them dearly.

They were all in my head.

The characters in the books could be whatever I wanted them to be. I could invent what they would look like. They started out kind of ghost-like, shimmering and ethereal, without any particular shape, size, or color. The more I read, the better I got at visualizing . . . putting clear images to the words. When I was growing up, there were almost no children's books with stories and characters that were black. But when I read a story about a girl and her adventures, it was very easy to see . . . in my mind . . . that she was brown and tall and skinny and looked just like me. I made myself the heroine. I traveled the world and went back and forth in time, got myself in trouble and got out of it again. And I never had to leave my house.

Reading was the joy of my life. It was something I could do alone. I wanted to read everything. Reading frequently made me laugh and, on occasion, cry. I could get angry, and even thoughtful, about some of what I was being told. But the most important thing was that reading always sent me on long dreamy airborne journeys, lifted and propelled on the wings of my own imagination.

It was through reading, in part, that I discovered that the world was much bigger than the Harlem neighborhood where I was raised, with many more different kinds of people than just my family and friends. Reading about other people, places, and things taught me to be curious. To want to know things . . . to want to learn. Being different was not only okay, it was desirable. I was to learn this fully as I grew up and recognized my own unique voice for storytelling. There was only one *me* in the whole world.

I did not know, when I was a child, that someday I would become a writer. When I sat down to begin my first book, it was simply, once again, to entertain myself. I set out to write new and different stories that I had not read before—stories with characters that looked like me, but also with characters of all different races because they reflected the real world I lived in. I wanted to create the kinds of adventures that keep readers turning pages to find out what happens in the end.

What I have come to see, from loving to read and to write, is that the willingness to suspend our disbelief, to look beyond where we are to what else is "out there," is part of the enjoyment and benefit of doing both. We can make ourselves happy and enlightened by the experience. Words that form stories, stories that talk about people, places, and things, are not the exclusive domain of any one culture, but belong to us all because they come from our hearts and minds. We find that our experiences are more the same than not—that imagination, dreams, hope, truth, and love don't come in colors. Color is a spin that is man-made.

When I go into a bookstore to look over the shelves of published materials, when I line up to get books autographed by authors or to hear them talk about their craft and stories, I am seeking not only to be entertained, but to venture into the writer's psyche. I want to pick their brains—and imagination—and be persuaded that the story they tell will be worth my time and attention.

One of the best gifts any of us can give a child, ours or someone else's, is an early introduction to reading. Take them to sign up for their very own library card, and encourage them to use it.

As an African American writer what I bring to the mix is a perspective on myself, others, the nation, and the world. The letters and support from readers are what affirms that what I write has successfully created that wonderful journey and fantasy that makes it worthwhile to pick up a book in the first place. Those adventures are possible because, as writers, we each have a unique story to tell. Our diversity is what makes us creatively strong, multifaceted, and talented. It keeps all of us fresh and on our toes. It offers us a wealth of possibilities. We can create our own acceptance or risk missing out on the free and readily available travels of a lifetime. Because it's really all in our heads.

REGIONAL BOOKSELLERS ASSOCIATIONS

For more information about independent bookstores in your area, please write to the regional association in the appropriate state or contact the American Booksellers Association.

Illinois, Indiana, Michigan, Ohio
> GREAT LAKES BOOKSELLERS ASSOCIATION
> Jim Dana (Executive Director)
> 509 Lafayette
> Grand Haven, MI 49417

Nevada, Utah
> INTERMOUNTAIN INDEPENDENT BOOKSELLERS ASSOCIATION
> Tony Weller (President)
> Sam Weller's Books
> 254 S. Main Street
> Salt Lake City, UT 84101

Houston Area, New Orleans-Gulf South, Oklahoma, and South-Central Booksellers Associations
> MID-SOUTH BOOKSELLERS ASSOCIATION
> Susan Daigre (President)
> Bookends
> P.O. Box 400, 111 Hwy. 90
> Bay St. Louis, MS 39520-0400

Arizona, Colorado, Nevada, New Mexico, Texas, Utah, Wyoming
　　MOUNTAINS & PLAINS BOOKSELLERS ASSOCIATION
　　Lisa Knudsen (Executive Director)
　　805 La Porte Ave.
　　Fort Collins, CO 80521

Delaware, Maryland, New Jersey, New York, Pennsylvania
　　NEW ATLANTIC INDEPENDENT BOOKSELLERS ASSOCIATION
　　Larry Robin (Executive Director)
　　Robin's Bookstore
　　108 S. 13th St.
　　Philadelphia, PA 19107

Connecticut, Maine, Massachusetts, New Hampshire, Rhode Island, Vermont
　　NEW ENGLAND BOOKSELLERS ASSOCIATION
　　Wayne "Rusty" Drugan (Executive Director)
　　847 Massachusetts Ave.
　　Cambridge, MA 02139

Louisiana, Mississippi, Oklahoma, Texas
　　NEW ORLEANS-GULF SOUTH BOOKSELLERS ASSOCIATION
　　Robert Schauffler (President)
　　P.O. Box 750043
　　New Orleans, LA 70175-0043

Northern California Area
　　NORTHERN CALIFORNIA INDEPENDENT BOOKSELLERS ASSOCIATION
　　Ginie Thorp and Hut Landon (Executive Directors)
　　5643 Paradise Dr., Suite 12
　　Corte Madera, CA 94925-1815

Oklahoma Area
　　OKLAHOMA INDEPENDENT BOOKSELLERS ASSOCIATION
　　Steve Stephenson (President)
　　Steve's Sundries
　　2612 S. Harvard
　　Tulsa, OK 74114

Alaska, Idaho, Montana, Oregon, Washington
    PACIFIC NORTHWEST BOOKSELLERS ASSOCIATION
    Thom Chambliss (Executive Director)
    1510 Mill St.
    Eugene, OR 97401-4258

San Diego Area
    SAN DIEGO BOOKSELLERS ASSOCIATION
    Brian Lucas (President)
    Adams Avenue Bookstore
    3502 Adams Ave.
    San Diego, CA 92116

Alabama, Arkansas, Florida, Georgia, Kentucky, Louisiana, Mississippi, North Carolina,
South Carolina, Tennessee, Virginia
    SOUTHEAST BOOKSELLERS ASSOCIATION
    Wanda Jewell (Executive Director)
    2730 Devine St.
    Columbia, SC 29205

Southern California Area
    SOUTHERN CALIFORNIA BOOKSELLERS ASSOCIATION
    Candace Moreno (President)
    P.O. Box 4176
    Culver City, CA 90231-4176

Illinois, Iowa, Kansas, Minnesota, Missouri, Nebraska, North Dakota, South Dakota,
Wisconsin
    UPPER MIDWEST BOOKSELLERS ASSOCIATION
    Susan Walker (Executive Director)
    5520 Park Pl.
    Edina, MN 55424

All other queries:
    AMERICAN BOOKSELLERS ASSOCIATION
    828 South Broadway
    Tarrytown, NY 10591

or visit our website at: http://www.bookweb.org

ACKNOWLEDGMENTS

Grateful acknowledgment is made to the following authors, illustrators, and publishers for their permission to reprint their pieces in *Out of the Mold* and to those who contributed original pieces for this book.

Book Race. Copyright © 1997 by Peter Sís.

Whichever. Copyright © 1996 by Jane Yolen. Printed with permission of Curtis Brown, Ltd.

Of Book Tours, Hell, and Possibilities. Copyright © 1997 by Connie May Fowler.

Preserving Our Stories. Copyright © 1996 by Richard Louv. From *The Web of Life: Weaving the Values That Sustain Us* by Richard Louv. Reprinted by permission of Conari Press.

Illustrations from Minty, A Story of Young Harriet Tubman. Copyright © 1996 by Jerry Pinkney. From *Minty, A Story of Young Harriet Tubman,* written by Alan Schroeder, published by Dial Books, a division of Penguin Books USA Inc.

Southern Quilts: Treasured "Kivver" for All. Copyright © 1996 by Clifton L. Taulbert. First appeared in *The Atlanta Constitution.*

To Whom the Angel Spoke: A Story of the Christmas. Copyright © 1991 by Terry Kay. Published by Peachtree Publishers. Reprinted by permission of the publisher.

Granddaughter. Copyright © 1996 by Jane Yolen. Printed with permission of Curtis Brown, Ltd.

Beyond the Divided States. Copyright © 1996 by Mark Gerzon. From *A House Divided: Six Belief Systems Struggling for America's Soul* by Mark Gerzon. Reprinted by permission of The Putnam Publishing Group/Jeremy P. Tarcher, Inc.

Children's Book. Copyright © 1997 by Peter Sís.

Required Reading and Other Dangerous Subjects. First appeared in *The Threepenny Review.* Reprinted by permission of Amy Tan and the Sandra Dijkstra Literary Agency.

The Moody Traveler. Copyright © 1996 by Phillip Lopate. First appeared in *The New York Times* and later in *Portrait of My Body*, An Anchor Book, published by Doubleday, a division of Bantam Doubleday Dell Publishing Group, Inc. Reprinted with permission.

The Island Light. Copyright © 1992 by Rosemary Wells. From *Voyage to the Bunny Planet* by Rosemary Wells. Used by permission of Dial Books for Young Readers, a division of Penguin Books USA Inc.

John Lewis. Copyright © 1970 by John Egerton. From *A Mind to Stay Here: Profiles from the South* by John Egerton, published by the Macmillian Company. Reprinted with permission.

Hair of the Dog {Siddalee, 1965}. From *Little Altars Everywhere* by Rebecca Wells, published by Broken Moon Press, 1992, reprinted by Harper Perennial, 1996.

Exchange of the Idea. Copyright © 1997 by Peter Sís.

Terrain of the Heart. Copyright © 1993 by Lee Smith. First appeared in *The News & Observer,* October 10, 1993.

It's All in Our Heads. Copyright © 1996 by Sandra Kitt.